Get On Google Front Page

SEO Tips for Online Marketing

Jason Matthews

Pismo Beach, California. USA

ISBN: 1456523546
EAN-13: 978-1456523541

Subjects include: SEO, SEO tips, Google, Bing, search engine optimization, online marketing, online business, internet marketing, internet business, e-commerce, e-business, keywords, keyword planner, blogs, blogging, alt text, metadata, page source and more.

Also by Jason Matthews

The Little Universe - a novel

Jim's Life - the sequel novel

Better You, Better Me - for a happy life

How to Make, Market and Sell Ebooks All for Free

How to Make Your Own Free Website: And Your Free Blog Too

This book is dedicated to
the website and blog owners
doing what they can
to help their sites perform better.

I know what it's like.

Table of Contents

Introduction

Why Google? Why focus on them and not just search engines in general? This is a valid question because there are Bing, Baidu, Ask, Entireweb and many others which shouldn't be ignored. If you research the global market share, you'll find different stats depending on region, month and validity of the source but one thing is consistent; *Google is the undisputed champion of the search engine world*, processing over a billion search requests daily. It will likely remain on top at least for a while.

On a global level, approximately 70% to 80% of all searches happen with Google (depending on who you believe) while the others combine to make up the final 20% to 30% (Sept. 2014). The stats also vary dramatically depending on the region. In some European countries Google holds over 90% of the market, an alarming number that may contribute to anti-trust law suits to prevent total domination of an industry. Additionally, they still dominate the mobile market share.

To be fair it's not quite so enormous in some countries, China for example. Baidu is the leader there though Google is not so distant at the number two spot with roughly one third of the market. People could argue the exact numbers but the point is moot. One thing that's clear to anyone promoting

1

themselves, a website or business online is that they must optimize for Google.

Because SEO (search engine optimization) is the best way for an absolute stranger to find any site with a search term, it can make or break an online business. Since it's crucial for internet success and also a largely misunderstood entity, some people pay large amounts of money for others to do SEO work for them. The truth is that many elements of SEO, especially the most important ones, can easily be done by you. What's more, *Google actually prefers websites that are promoted organically with natural, ethical and un-paid efforts.* This is great news for website owners, people just starting out or those with smaller budgets for marketing.

Anyone can do SEO work effectively for free, and anyone can get on Google's front page.

Several years ago I didn't know anything about SEO and most of the verbiage was foreign. As a result it seemed like the only way to accomplish anything online for my business ideas was to hire someone else to do it. And so I paid professional webdesigners to create webpages promoting my businesses which soon became frustrating and expensive. I spent thousands of dollars on four different pros to build four different sites: three websites and one blog. In each case they did their best to interpret my concepts and come up with sites that worked for me.

Surprisingly, some of these professional webdesigners didn't know much more than I did about maximizing SEO efforts. They also charged anywhere from $45 to $120 per hour. Ouch! As very few visitors showed up, it became evident that I still had to market the websites. That meant blogging, submitting articles, building links, learning page source elements and more. *Just because a pro builds your website, there's no guarantee people will visit.* I learned that effort was needed to drive traffic. Nobody was going to do that for me or help with SEO unless I also wanted to pay more money.

And the painful lesson *was discovering that I could have done a better job myself for free.* It wasn't complicated. I could have done a fine job with SEO, good enough for my needs, everything it took to rise to the top page of Google. I just didn't know that back then.

Those days are over. Now if I have an idea that requires an online presence, I just make the website or blog myself and figure out what to do to get it to rise to the first page of a search. It does take some time but not too much.A The best parts are that it's actually fairly easy and entirely free. In fact, my sites have made it to Google's front page for well over 1,000 different search terms at the time of this writing.

The only requirement is a bit of time, and you too can get on Google's front page.

Plus it's fun. You'll get a real kick seeing a search result on or near the top that points to one of your websites or products.

Preliminary Remarks

Just to make things clear, *I don't know advanced HTML coding* (webpage language), and you won't have to master it to succeed at this. A little bit, yes. A lot, no. The good news is you don't have to. Great SEO results can be had by anybody with basic understanding of it, which is explained in this book. You also don't need huge traffic coming to visit. The tips that follow will get you on page one, and then the traffic will come in and help even more.

But before we get to all of the instruction that follows, let me mention a few things. First, the order in which you do the coming tips is not mandatory to be done in sequence, with the exception of the *keyword research where it all begins*. You can do the rest in several orders and still succeed. I also recommend you read through this **entirely** before getting entrenched in any one area. It's not a big book but it is packed with information. Read through it first, then you'll have a clearer idea on the whole scheme of things.

Second, I'm going to present you with a wealth of information. For some, much of this will be new; for others there will be parts that feel like a review. All of it has to do with online methods for accomplishing your goals, so those who are less familiar with the internet and their computers may at times feel overwhelmed. Not to worry, *feeling overwhelmed by this is a natural response and something I've experienced plenty of times.* For those who feel inundated by this, please think of it as a diet or exercise program. *All you need to do is a little bit each day.* Follow these tips, and I promise that you'll rise dramatically in a Google search and eventually will get to the very first page.

There are always tutorials that will go into great detail on any one of these tips I'm about to share. YouTube.com (owned by Google and 2nd largest search engine) is an excellent place to watch videos that explain more fully how to do these things. I will touch on them all, some in more depth than others, but if you still need extra info just go to YouTube or do an internet search with "tutorial on *the subject you're looking for.*" I do this frequently, even for the research to write this book.

Also know that Google routinely changes their algorithm, up to hundreds of changes per year. Most are minor while some are major adjustments, like Penguin and Panda. Since the algorithm remains a secret, it's wise for webmasters to focus on the simple recommendations from Google and providing great content rather than worrying endlessly about every single detail of their website's SEO factors.

Finally, if any customer of this book would also like a free pdf version that might be handier on her/his computer with all the active hyperlinks, just let me know. I don't have any way of verifying who bought the book through a retailer other than if she/he left a review, so if that sounds fair just direct me to the review and receive a free pdf copy. It is wise to give it a quick read first, then leave a review and get your free pdf with all the hyperlinks. Email jason@thelittleuniverse.com with *free pdf for my review* in the subject box.

Creating Quality Content

It's been said a million times because it's true. *Content is king.* The single most important thing anyone can do to help them rise in SER (search engine ranking) is to create and/or deliver quality content. In fact, a website could make absolutely no effort to enhance SEO factors and still be incredibly popular if it just has excellent content. Why? Because the visitors will still come, recommend the site to others, link to it, write articles about it, essentially do all the SEO work for it.

This often gets overlooked, but it's the foundation for online success. The more value a website has to users, the more traffic it gets, the more time visitors spend there, the more others will link to it, the more click-throughs happen, the lower the bounce rate (visitors leaving after seeing the landing page)... everything is made better by having good content on a website.

Google prides itself on developing a complex algorithm with over 200 variables that *attempts to match searchers with websites that have the content they're looking for.* This means Google really cares about user-friendly sites with high authority content delivering on the search terms they say they're delivering on. This also means that Google does not like sites that are stuffed with keywords and provide little or no real value to the user. In fact, Google does not like such sites, and this gets into Black Hat SEO practices which we'll discuss in a moment. To make Google happy, you want to create websites with excellent content that make users happy, plus you can use the White Hat tips I'm about to share.

Google keeps space open for search results that have not been paid for. This is excellent news! Sponsored ads run on the side of the search results page. Sometimes a few paid ads also run at the top of the main body (shaded with a different background color), but the rest are free, organically produced search results. Again this means that anybody can get to page one and Google actually leaves room for them at the top.

First and foremost, your goal should be to provide a valuable user experience. And so here's the opening Get On Google Front Page Step to take:

GOGFP Step #1. Provide great content. Make your website the very best it can be so others will visit, spend time, share and link to it.

This is easier said than done. Obviously it's critical to optimize the items within your own control. The text must read well and be informative or entertaining. The images should be real eye-catchers. Video must be interesting and typically not too long. Everything that you provide must be at its very best. But what else can you do?

Here's a brief list of things you can add to a site to create more quality for any visitor:

- Link to existing articles on your subject. Find supplemental information and provide it as a helpful gesture. Places like EzineArticles are perfect for this and allow reuse with proper crediting.

- Add video whether it's yours or someone else's. Most people like having their videos shared as long as it's clear they are credited for it.

- Include interviews with authorities in the field or people of interest.

- Create a forum page encouraging questions and/or answers for anything related.

- Offer a Links page to other webmasters for mutual benefit, especially those that complement your work. It's like partnering with others who can help reciprocally.

- Include a database for further research.

- Add widgets that are informative or entertaining. The Blog Widgets is a good place for that. http://www.theblogwidgets.com/

Make an effort to provide visitors with as much value, information, entertainment, etc. so they will stay at your site, enjoy it, subscribe to it, recommend it and link to it. That alone will make your SEO life so much easier.

SEO (search engine optimization), what exactly is it again?

Simply defined, SEO is the act of assisting the search engines to find your website and thus improving the status of your ranking. Most people only look at the top page worth of results after typing a search term, and very few people scroll beyond the second or third page. So any search engine success is greatly affected by your ability to be on the first page and to stay there. Hence the need for smart SEO practices.

Google is well aware of this and spends much effort to educate users with literature and video on how to do this in ways that are both beneficial and done with integrity (or White Hat).

From Google's SEO Starter Guide;

Search engine optimization is often about making small modifications to parts of your website. When viewed individually, these changes might seem like incremental improvements, but when combined with other optimizations, they could have a noticeable impact on your site's user experience and performance in organic search results.

It's the job of search engines to find sites matching the criteria that people are looking for. Obviously it's best if search engines list your site as a place of interest for anyone using terms related to your subjects. To begin, you'll almost surely start out deep in their results, like on page 20, but over time you'll climb ever closer to the first page by adhering to the advice that follows. Eventually you will make it to page one.

Years ago when I first created an internet presence and searched for my own name, I came up on page 17 and felt discouraged. In time I slowly climbed closer to page one even though my name is fairly common. There are approximately 600 people in the US with the name "Jason Matthews." Worldwide there are perhaps 800. Many of these people are referenced online, and in a "name branding" way we're all in competition with each other to be on the first page. Fortunately, my websites now experience decent search results for my name and, more importantly, for my subjects of interest. I will talk later about not only optimizing for your subjects but also branding yourself.

Although in a funny way, you don't need to worry about the search engines finding your website. They will find it; I guarantee that. To know immediately if they've found it or not, simply type in the entire URL into the search box as in http://example.com and see if it comes up at the top of the list. If it's not there, have no fear. It usually takes up to two weeks before they index a site. Give it some time and try again. I'll instruct how to submit your sites directly to Google and many other search engines, but even if you don't they will still find it. How do I know? Because Google Alerts is set up to notify me on subjects like my name, books, the download pages for my ebooks, etc., whenever anybody on Earth posts something on those items. It doesn't seem to matter how trivial or tiny the posting or the website is; like the concept of

George Orwell's Big Brother, Google knows what's happening in Cyberworld.

However, you absolutely do want to maximize the recognition of search engines like Google and Bing *to not only find you but to associate the site with what you're trying to accomplish.* That means not only does Google see your site specializing in African coffee, for example, but that it believes you really know everything about African coffee because of the factors Google considers important. There are many ways to help in this regard, *but remember this takes time.* Search engine indexes also place value on visitor numbers, inbound links and how long a site has been in existence, and they prefer established sites with lots of data, incoming links and recorded visits over newer ones. Be patient and give it time as in weeks to months or sometimes even a year. As long as you stay diligent with the advice that follows, your sites will climb in the rankings slowly but surely.

GOGFP Step # 2. Be patient and treat SEO like a diet or exercise program. It takes time, and the results will be great if you remain persistent.

Remember; I'm about to share the central SEO tips, the same factors that got me to Google's first page in a short time. Please remember that these are basically shared in order of importance. *In general, the ones at the beginning are more important than the tips at the end.* That's been true for me so please put most of your emphasis on the beginning SEO tips, although they each are important and will vary depending on an individual's needs.

Keyword Research,
Where You Must Begin

Keywords are essential to help search engines link your sites to certain words, terms or phrases. Keywords can be individual words like "diet" or "weight loss," a set of words like "healthy weight loss," or even phrases containing many words such as "eat all you want and still lose weight." This is also the difference between short-tail and long-tail keywords, or the difference between targeting broad markets under heavy competition from other advertisers versus niche markets with less competition. It's best to add keywords (both short-tail and long) to every site, blog, URL, title, article, image and location that has boxes for them, keywords that describe the content of what your information is about. But before we get into the details of how and where to insert keywords, we're going to discuss at length how to discover which are your very best keywords.

Your best keywords describe your website content and are being searched by lots of people with relatively low competition.

Okay, that was a mouthful but true. Certain keywords will only help if people are actually searching for them, and your site is relevant to that subject, and (hopefully) there is not a ton of competition. If the competition is low, then you're golden and the climb to the front page can be quick. If the competition is high, you can still get to the top but it will take great SEO habits and more time.

Start by making a list of possible keywords and phrases that describe your business, website, service, book, product, whatever it is you need to market. Let this list be as long as you want because a few hours of initial keyword research will help immensely in SEO efforts over time.

The extra hours spent determining the very best keywords equates to greater likelihood of reaching the top spots in far fewer weeks.

Let's use a fictional example for how to get started. Let's say that Linda Marshall saw a UFO as a child and has spent her life pursuing this field. Linda wants to write a book and build a website for her study on UFOs. She has collected hundreds of photographs, dozens of videos, stories from eye-witnesses and even people claiming to have been abducted, everything that has to do with the entire UFO phenomenon. Linda's book is half finished, and she also plans to host a blog, market t-shirts, coffee mugs, etc. She hasn't made a final decision on the book title or that of the website but has some thoughts.

Now it's time to come up with an array of ideas for Linda's keywords and keyword phrases. These should be both short-tail and long-tail terms. Short-tail terms are competitive, broad ranging and typically one, two or three words. Long-tail terms are more specific and can be several words or a phrase. Remember that lower or upper case letters don't matter to search engines. Here's a partial list:

UFO
UFOs
Unidentified flying object
I saw a UFO and nobody believes me

Flying saucer

Spacecraft

Aliens

Alien abduction cases

Alien abduction stories

Alien abductions

Extraterrestrial

Extraterrestrial intelligence

Men from mars

I went for a ride in a UFO

Encounters of the fourth kind

Close encounters of the fourth kind

UFO pictures

UFO sightings

SETI

Search for extraterrestrial life

And so on and so on. Obviously this list could become quite long but that's okay. *Linda should write down just about anything that comes to mind* so she can then research what the results for those search terms are as well as the results for similar terms.

Fortunately our research is made easy because Google has a very helpful program called Keyword Planner (formerly Keyword Tool) at this link - http://adwords.google.com/keywordplanner. There you need to sign up for a free AdWords account and then type in certain words or phrases and follow the links for **Keyword Ideas** or **Get Ideas** to research how many times per month Google actually receives that exact request for information. (Notice the results from searches change each month as these things fluctuate like the stock market.) You'll also see how much competition there is from others using those same keywords. *Ideally, you can find keywords that have low competition from other advertisers and a high number of searches from users each month.*

Back to Linda's example. The first thing I notice is that the term "UFO" gets 823,000 global monthly searches (as of Sept. 2014) and has low competition which is outstanding! The plural of the term, "UFOs," also has low competition from other advertisers, but it only gets around 60,500 monthly searches. Actually that number is enormous too and generally would be fantastic, but in this case it would be smarter to use the singular "UFO." Entirely spelling out the words, "Unidentified flying object" just gets 2,400 searches which could be considered a good long-tail keyword choice.

The word "aliens" gets 450,000 monthly searches while "extraterrestrial intelligence" gets just 720. Plus the second phrase is so likely to be misspelled that this choice is a no-brainer. However "aliens" can also refer to foreigners so that needs to be recognized. Check this type of question by either clicking on the listed keyword or typing "aliens" into a Google search. Since the top results are entirely about visitors from outer space, that's comforting (at least for Linda).

Let's compare "ufo sightings" verses "ufo pictures." It sounds like a fair match, but the first phrase gets 110,000 searches per month with low competition while the second phrase only gets 6,600 searches and has similar competition. Again we see that "ufo sightings" is smarter than "ufo pictures," and "ufo sighting" (singular) is not as good as the plural.

"Alien abduction cases" gets 1,000 monthly searches. "Alien abduction stories" gets 5,400. "Alien abductions" gets

4,400. Since they all have low competition, I'd recommend the one with the most results.

An analysis of "flying saucer" and "spacecraft" shows us that they both have similar search numbers. In cases like this, I'd prefer the term that most resembles what Linda has to offer, which is called **relevance.** Since the results from a "spacecraft" search are dominated by NASA projects, I'd pick "flying saucer." On this note "flying saucer stories" and "flying saucer reports" do not get searched enough to have data shown, but "flying saucer photos" does get 140 per month. It's small but better than nothing, and it is a huge part of her website and book.

What's incredibly helpful is that Google will automatically provide other similar terms you might not think of but are often excellent substitutes. In Linda's case, scrolling through those results showed me that "Area 51" and "UFO news" are hugely popular terms and relevant for what Linda has to offer.

There are also ways of filtering the results and asking Google for certain parameters. Here are some quick tips to use this service even better:

- A left side tab allows you to filter results by location (global or by nations, cities, region), language and for Google or all its partners too. a number of choices including relevance, competition, global monthly searches and more.
- For some people, like dentists or businesses where physical presence is required, the local monthly search results will be more important than the global searches.

- You can also filter for Approximate Cost per Click if you ever decide to pay for front page listings. This is entirely optional, *not at all mandatory for SEO*, but if you find a cheap option like 50 cents or less per click, it might be worth it. The tab gives even more insight to the real competition for those keywords, as in the lower a price the better.

- On the menu you can filter for matches that are Broad matches, Exact matches or Phrase matches that affect click and cost estimates should you decide to pay for an ad campaign.

- Advanced Options allows you to select Locations, Languages and to apply other filters.

- You can Include or Exclude certain words to customize results of ideas from Google.

- Instead of a keyword you can input a website URL to see which keywords they are coming up for in searches to do homework on the other guys.

For many people, it's most important to focus on the basic categories of Global Monthly Searches and Competition level. From there, you'll get what you really need and then can play around with further inquiries.

Back to our fictional example of Linda Marshall. If I also select the search to list by order of Global Monthly searches, it will be clear which ones are Linda's best keywords. A brief study of her search terms would lead to a partial list in this order or *basically* in this order depending on what she's focusing on:

UFO

Aliens

Area 51

UFO news

UFO sightings

Flying saucer

Alien abduction stories

Linda Marshall

I've included "Linda Marshall" because it's often important to brand yourself along with your subjects. Additionally, nearly 720 monthly searches occur for that name, so Linda will need to make an effort to stand out from the other Linda Marshalls of the world. (If branding yourself or a product, like an invention, is the primary goal then your name and those terms will be high on your keyword list.)

At this point, these are all short-tail keywords. They will be best for Linda's URL, page titles, book title, meta description and other areas, though we need to recognize some long-tail keywords also. The best long-tail results will get used in page text content, blogs, articles, press releases and more. Here are some of the long-tail terms, especially when used with other wording, that Linda will want to store for later:

New UFO sightings

Videos of aliens

Latest UFO reports

Pictures of an alien

Additionally, Linda can include locations like "Arizona Desert" or other descriptions like "Annunaki return" that will be reserved for articles, blog posts, blog titles and other places where long-tail keywords are most effective.

These will be some of Linda's main keywords for the website, book, blog and more, as she'll benefit by sprinkling them into everything she does. For examples, her URL domain name might be http://www.ufo-aliens.com and book title might be *UFO News and Alien Abduction Stories*. She might make multiple blog posts and submit articles with titles like *"Grey Aliens over the Arizona Desert"* and *"Why the Annunaki are Returning to New Mexico."*

Now that Linda knows both short and long-tail keywords, she can design her URL, book title and anything content-related to her subjects. This will surely help **Google and people** find her over time.

We've learned the next most important step of SEO efforts. *You must use the Keyword Planner to discover which terms are relevant, most commonly searched and have lower competition.* Hopefully you can use relevant and highly searched words that others aren't using. After doing keyword planner research you should have a list of at least six to ten optimized keywords and phrases.

GOGFP Step #3. Use the Keyword Planner to optimize at least 6 to 10 keyword terms. These should be both short and long-tail to be used later accordingly.

Short-tail keywords are mostly going to be used in your URL domain name, meta description, page titles and within your text and page body. Long-tail keywords are mostly going to be used in your meta description, blog titles, page titles, articles submitted, press releases and comment boxes. There is an overlap effect for short-tail and long-tail keywords, as the short-tail are more related to headline type things while the long-tail are more related to textual body type things. This will make more sense as we get into it.

I have been marketing a short-tail term for about two years, **sell ebooks,** since I teach writers to make and sell ebooks. Even though the monthly search numbers are not astronomical, it's a highly competitive term. Currently my sites or Amazon book fluctuate in and out of the top page results. However, a huge number of closely related long-tail keywords list my sites or book on page one (or they have in the past). These are terms I didn't plan for but just happened naturally through blogging, submitting articles and from text on my websites. This is a very partial list:

sell ebooks wordpress

how to make and sell ebooks

sell ebooks automated system

create a blog to sell ebooks

web pages to sell ebooks

best sites to buy or sell ebooks

how much does it cost to sell ebooks on Amazon

sell ebooks as a minor

build a website to sell ebooks

sell ebooks on iPad

how to sell ebooks on Facebook

best place to sell ebooks

websites already built to sell ebooks

I want to start a blog and sell ebooks can someone teach me

It can be humorous, and the true list is far too long to even mention. Over time, all of these search terms have lead people to my blog on selling ebooks. Some terms will still get my site on page one while others have dropped down. It's important to recognize a few things here:

- It would be impossible and foolish to attempt to market all of these long-tail keywords. Don't try too hard with long-tails; they tend to work themselves out.

- Even though I'm not on the first page for several short-tails, I am on page one for a huge number of closely related long-tails. In time this will help my chances of a page one result for the coveted short-tails.

- After two years of doing this, I wasn't quite on page one for a highly competitive short-tail term, but I was there for dozens of similar terms and finally made it to page one. Don't worry if you experience similar results. Short-tail and competitive terms take longer, while less competition and long-tails can be a very quick climb to the top.

Now you understand how to find your keywords. Very soon we'll discuss where and how to implement them on your blog, website and more. But first I want to briefly discuss some methods of SEO called White Hat versus Black Hat tactics. This is a subject that can either make Google very happy or could even get your site banned from their index.

White Hat vs. Black Hat Methods
and What to Beware of

White Hat versus Black Hat sounds like a climax scene in a Western movie. Everyone knows the good guys wear the white hats, right? Although this is a huge subject for SEO where we could spend a lot of time, I'd like to cover only a few items to watch out for since most people never go near the majority of Black Hat tactics. *However, even with ethical, organic methods it is often a fine line and sometimes hard to tell just which hat you're wearing.*

Understanding how Google works has led many webdesigners to attempt manipulation of the process. Over the years, dozens of unethical methods have been designed to fool the robot spiders (Google's search force or Googlebots) into ranking a certain site very high when, in actuality, it is not worthy of high ranking but just trying to cut corners and trick visitors into coming over for whatever reason.

Like any business, Google wants people to enjoy its service and results. Therefore Google promotes websites that practice methods consistent with ethics, integrity and organic means, or natural and un-paid ways of associating themselves with their keywords. This is known as White Hat SEO versus Black Hat SEO. White Hat is good and makes Google happy. Black Hat is bad and can get a site banned from being indexed. I will run through a short list of the ones you're most likely to encounter so you'll know what to do and what not to do.

Please beware; there is sometimes a very fine line between optimizing your site and using Black Hat techniques.

Keyword Stuffing.

Have you ever seen a website that contained the same words repeated unnaturally throughout a page? It's horribly unpleasant to read, and the webdesigner is trying to make the search engines think that webpage is an absolute authority on "running shoes" for example, because the words "running shoes" come up dozens of times on a single page. The page might read like this:

Welcome to running shoes site where our brands running shoes are guaranteed running shoes to put you in a pair of running shoes that look and running shoes feel great. Our prices running shoes are among the lowest running shoes around...

That would be keyword stuffing. A similar example of Black Hat use of keywords is adding "running shoes" multiple times to the metadata description which we'll discuss more in a later chapter.

Unfortunately it's often a fine line between optimizing your site for keywords and stuffing them. If you honestly do sell running shoes then you should have that term in the meta description, URL, page title and several times within the body of the webpages. So how do you know what's search engine optimizing and what's keyword stuffing?

Great question! The consensus seems to be that anything more than one or two mentions of it directly in the meta description is too much and more than five ways of saying varied phrases with the same keywords is too much as in "great running shoes," "running shoes for men," "running shoes for women," cheap running shoes," "quality running shoes," "all sizes running shoes," and so on would be Black Hat in your metadata or even a body of text without much more verbiage.

A safe rule of thumb is to think about the user experience and keep it pleasant.

So a White Hat method of using these keywords slightly different throughout the page text as "running shoes," "running sneakers," "athletic shoes," "sports shoes," "running gear," "track cleats," and so on. The words "running shoes" can also appear in the meta description, URL, page heading, title of page and repeated a few times in the page body. It can also be highlighted once or twice in **bold** in the page body.

Google treats its algorithm like Coca Cola keeps its list of ingredients: one majorly guarded secret. The Google algorithm is top secret so unscrupulous people don't know exactly where the lines are drawn and must play it on the safe side. The bottom line is this—we'll go over how to repeat your keywords tastefully without stuffing them, but always think of the user experience and keep it pleasant.

Hidden or Invisible Text.

This is text that's invisible to a human but visible to computers. Hidden text can be written either transparent or in the same color as the page background so it's invisible to us, but the computers see it in the coding of the page. For example, the word "sex" might be hidden and come up dozens of time on a page. That's because many people search the term and would likely find your site, click for a visit and then perhaps find something else they wanted, like running shoes. So search engines have learned to deal with hidden text, and you are highly advised not to use any even though I doubt you would.

Doorway and Cloaked Pages.

This is a technique that basically presents a different picture to the search engine spiders as it does to the actual webpage visitor, or it redirects visitors to somewhere else than where they thought they were going. I see no need to go into great detail on this one because you should never even deal with this if you are promoting a website in ethical manners. Even if you use a 301 redirect (which we'll discuss later) to lead visitors to a new URL name, the content would be what they had planned for. *In general, don't try to fool anyone: the spiders or your visitors.*

Comment Spam.

Later when we discuss methods of getting your URL backlinks out there, we'll talk about leaving comments on other people's blogs and articles with links back to yours. This can be done either ethically or unethically. Ethical methods involve leaving thoughtful comments about the actual post in ways that add to the overall experience. Unethical methods involve copying and pasting the same message to many posts or leaving a comment and URL link that has nothing to do with the article. We will practice the White Hat technique of regularly commenting on other people's blogs with backlinks but not spamming. As with using keywords, this is one SEO area where there are many shades of gray.

Link Farming or Spamdexing.

This is when a group of websites are all listed on each other's sites and each points back to every other site, creating a huge network of related sites in the eyes of search engines. While it is a perfectly acceptable White Hat method to have several websites, each linking to the others, it is not ethical to engage in building multiple websites whose primary purpose is to fabricate such extravagant networks. *You may be tempted to pay for services that promise thousands of instant incoming one-way links* guaranteed to boost your "popularity" with search engines, but this is actually a Black Hat technique to beware of.

A White Hat method would be to share links with others over time, links to similar websites and with friends, family, blog owners and others you'd like to support on a reciprocal basis.

There are plenty more, but I doubt you'll encounter them. In general, Black Hat methods are a fast-track attempt to get high rankings quickly without providing a quality user experience. White Hat methods usually take longer, but they are much safer and can still work great. Because anyone who wants to truly succeed online must be prepared to be in it for the duration with quality content, I will only recommend methods which are White Hat.

Deciding on a Domain Name

Perhaps you already have a website and/or a blog, perhaps not. If not, that's great because you definitely want to consider *adding keywords to the domain name*. If you already have a site, then it should be determined if your current URL is helping with SEO. We're about to talk at length about choosing the right domain name, and for some people it may be a difficult decision to stay with what they have or to make a change.

If your current website is established or doing well with page rank and traffic, you'll probably want to leave it as it is. But if it's not doing well, then a decision can be made whether to work around the existing domain name or to start over with a new URL that is *domain name optimized*. This is entirely up to you. I know that type of change sounds unpleasant, but if the existing URL is not keyword-rich and the site gets very little traffic, then it should be seriously considered. At first a change like this can briefly hurt SEO results as it can be like starting over. But if the current site is not performing well, would starting over be so bad especially if every aspect of the new site is wisely optimized? Within just a few weeks or months a new site that is *domain name optimized* will greatly outperform one that isn't. And by using a 301 redirect (which we'll discuss) the transition can be simple without damaging past SEO results.

I realized this far too late in my own internet career, after already creating a few websites and feeling like I had to stick with their existing domain name, which I did. In fact, I still feel that way and often think of better URL addresses because *this is one of the most important elements of SEO.*

The lesson here is that **keywords in your URL** really help! In fact, *the URL alone might be the most important place to add short-tail keywords or for name branding.* It can get you to Google's front page even if you don't ever mention those keywords in the text body or meta description. Experiment with Google searches for a wide variety of keywords, and see how often the first page results have those keywords in the URL. You might be surprised. Please read this paragraph again if you didn't understand the gravity of the concept.

GOGFP Step #4. This is arguably the most important lesson. Optimize your URL domain name to include your best short-tail keywords. It's okay if these keywords are competitive since you are in this for the duration.

"Terrific," you say sarcastically, "what if my domain name is already set and not optimized?"

Please don't shoot the messenger, but the URL domain name is one of the most important elements of SEO. That has been the case with my sites and many other high-ranking results when I do searches. However, if your URL is already set and it enjoys decent traffic with good page ranking (a zero to 9 scale that can be checked here - http://www.checkpagerank.net/ anything 3 or more being pretty good), established name branding, etc., then you can stick with the existing URL. In a later chapter we'll go through explanations for 301 URL redirects for those with sites that aren't doing well and want to make this change. And for people who are not willing to change, I can understand because some of my sites are also not domain name optimized and they feel too established to modify now. *The good news is you can still make it to page one of Google without a domain name optimized URL.* The bad news is that it will take longer, and it might never get as high as it could have. For those who wish to consider this change, especially if the current URL is not experiencing great results, please read the part 2 section on 301 URL redirects.

Back to the lesson for those creating a new URL and/or site. As explained, it helps dramatically if the words in the URL domain name are related to any possible internet search terms for someone looking for what you have to offer (e.g., solarbirdbath.com). That would be a wise URL if someone wanted a solar powered birdbath with a fountain and heated water, and so they searched online by typing the phrase "solar birdbath." It's actually a term which gets typed into Google searches 1,900 times per month as of Sept. 2014.

However, you might already have a name in mind like "cutelittlebirdiebath.com." While the phrase fills my heart with joy, that term gets zero monthly searches and won't help much with SEO. If that's the name, cutelittlebirdiebath.com, then you'll have to continually work harder at optimizing every other aspect of the site and will never reach the full potential for people conducting a keyword search for what they really want: a solar birdbath.

While cutelittlebirdiebath.com is a catchy phrase, ultimately the site might be stuck on page two or three. That would cause it to miss out on thousands of potential visitors every month, absolute strangers who searched the term "solar birdbath" and clicked on a higher ranking competitor.

For another example, let me explain how I came to decide on the title for this book and the URL of the website. This book is about teaching others to rise organically with Google to the top page. Back when making early decisions, I wrote down the major keywords and phrases that came to mind. Here's the partial list:

Rise on Google

Google first page

First page of Google

Google top page

Page one Google

Google page one

Front page Google

How to get on the first page of Google

And so on and so on. Then I went to Keyword Planner and checked these phrases. They can be done individually or many at once. The program automatically provides similar terms for making comparisons among slightly different words and phrases.

I saw that "Google front page" and "get on Google" were popular search terms with little competition. (Results below are very different since Keyword Tool has been replaced by Keyword Planner.) In January 2011, "get on Google" had 246,000 broad monthly searches while "Google front page" had 135,000. So by combining the two phrases into my book title of "Get On Google Front Page" I applied my title to a possible 381,000 broad monthly searches. In my opinion this was much smarter than calling the book "Get On **The** Front Page **Of** Google" because those extra article words will reduce the exact match of the search terms. While it's true that it reads slightly awkward, the phrase should translate to more visitors and book sales.

Also recognize that "Google start page" got 20% more local searches than "Google front page," and they both had equally low competition. That's a modest difference which I can live with if it makes the title more pleasant. These are decisions you'll likely make too, so weigh everything carefully and proceed.

Back to this example. In less than an hour I had narrowed the book title and website URL down to this: "Get On Google Front Page." I then checked availability at a domain name registrar and the website hosting company where I wanted to create a free example for this book. Both were available so I registered the name as a pure dot com and also went ahead and registered it as getongooglefrontpage.webs.com because I like having free websites. (Know this; a freely hosted website usually has the extra suffix, and a change to a pure dot com or other suffix is only about $10 per year. I have both versions of domain names: free and custom, but the custom domain names admittedly do better with search engines so you will probably want a custom domain name.)

Finally, I wanted to name the book, *Get On Google Front Page*. I went to Amazon and typed that into a book search. I was delighted to see no one had a book with that title. Surprisingly, there were very few titles even close to it, so I knew this would be a great name for people to find my website and the Amazon book. This way the keywords are part of the URL address and book title, and **over time** people will certainly find them with search engine terms.

These terms are typically short-tail keywords that will have competition. I'm in it for the duration, so that's okay. My long-tail keywords will come up in blog posts, text of pages and articles.

The Hidden Benefit of Free Websites and Other Dot Suffixes.

I've written a book specifically on making free websites and blogs because I enjoy doing things myself and love to save money whenever possible. It's called, *How to Make Your Own Free Website: And Your Free Blog Too* and will help anyone get the most of that experience.

There's another reason I like free websites, or would consider a suffix other than dot com, and after playing around with keyword searches the reason is fairly obvious. While many keyword-rich URLs are impossible to get the standard way, as in http://runningshoes.com, they are often readily available with either a free website or a non-standard suffix such as http://runningshoes.wordpress.com or http://runningshoes.net.

There are several other suffixes including .info, .org, .net, .biz, .co, .us, .ca, .me, .tv, .mobi and others. Despite certain requirements of the past, like .org being for non-profit organizations, there are almost no restrictions on any of them anymore.

There are also plenty of places for free blogs and websites where you can often get the exact URL you want provided the domain is followed by a subdomain, like one of my websites, http://your-own-free-website.webs.com. Using a different suffix or free site like this could help you get literally any domain name, even something like http://jamesjohnson.ws.

The main downside to that choice is the domain host, Wordpress for example, will be benefiting more than the site itself. A custom domain name for $10 per year would help fix that.

Also there are some people that claim a free website or different suffix makes a site look unprofessional. I disagree. Unprofessional looking sites are that way because the owner didn't put the time and care into making them better. If you have a product or information that people really want, they won't care if your site is freely hosted or if it ends in .info.

For those who already have a website and believe the URL domain name is not optimized, they may consider building a new site and doing a 301 permanent redirect from the old domain name to the new one. If the old site gets very little traffic and low page rank, then why not? For others this can be a tough choice and not a plan to go into lightly. I've included more info for a 301 Redirect (Optional) in the chapter on Fix the Problems.

Power of Blogs and Blogging

While most everyone recognizes the need for a website to promote a business, service or product, many people underestimate the power of a blog.

Blogging on a regular basis is one of the best things a webmaster can do to boost SEO results over time.

The reason is because you can do just about anything with a blog. Any subject can be covered, even things unrelated to your main purpose. You can get creative, share photos, links, videos from other sources (often) more so than on your regular website. Blogs are also perfect for incorporating content from other people, and they'll have interest in sending traffic your way. It's also a great place to benefit unexpectedly from long-tail keywords.

Let me share a brief and partial list of short and long-tail keywords that visitors have searched then found my blogs on Google's first page. Not only did they see my link, but they clicked on it. It's funny since I had no intention of ever making the front page for many of these listings. They just happened to be something I wrote articles about and either had the subject in the heading, page body, categories, tags or some combination. Here's a very partial list from two blogs; one I've used since 2008, the other since 2010:

2epub

pixel of ink

kindle

uploadnsell

nike neon yellow socks

german people

average life expectancy of nfl players

html codes on youtube channels

smashwords ibookstore

black kickers in the nfl

doc to epub

createspace ebook

Oregon ducks yellow socks

2epub converter

how to sell ebooks on wordpress

sell ebooks on wordpress

jana m

selling ebooks from your website google

word to epub

jesse ventura haarp

smashwords pubit or amazon?

2epub review

can i sell stuff wordpress free blogs

reviews on avatar as a spirtually fiction movie

*.doc to *.mobi

wordpress sell ebooks

sell ebook wordpress theme

create space ebook

how to upload free ebooks with your ebook

how selling ebooks on ibookstore

free translations widgets for woldpress

make a website and publish it for free never have to pay
at all not a penney

google ebook selling

what will happen to my ebooks when barnes and noble is sold/

selling ebooks, automated system

how to create an ebook facebook page

google editions ebooks3 selling ebooks on nook

best sites to buy or sell ebooks

This partial list represents visitors who saw my blog on page one results of Google. (There are well over 1,000 search terms that have led visitors to my blogs in just the last year. Also recognize that some of these terms will still land a searcher on page one while others are currently nowhere near the top as results are constantly in flux.)

The terms are primarily long-tail keywords. Believe me, most were complete surprises. The results were the product of simply blogging regularly on things I found interesting.

The power of blogging regularly results in visitors finding your site for many terms that will surprise you.

Also notice there are misspellings in the search terms, or how many incomplete entries exist, or wrongly worded entries. It would be impossible to intentionally optimize these mutated variations for SEO purposes. With a blog, just focus on writing weekly posts covering your subjects of interest and like-minded people will find the site. For this reason *I want to discuss the need to create a blog in addition to a website or even instead of a website for some people.*

GOGFP Step #5. Blog regularly, weekly or bi-weekly if you can. Even brief posts under 400 words will lead visitors to any site. Use short-tail keywords for categories, tags and labels, while using long-tail keywords for the titles of posts and the accompanying text.

A lot of people have no idea how important a blog site can be to their online platform. You can think of your blog as the nerve center, the one area that leads to everything else online about you. It's essential to maximize online presence. Fortunately, there are free places to create a blog. Notice, for the free domain name your site will have a URL like domainname.wordpress.com or domainname.blogger.com, but you can upgrade to a custom URL for about $10/year which will help with SEO in time. One of my blogs, http://ebooksuccess4free.wordpress.com is very successful with search engines and converting customers, even though the domain name is long and not a pure dot com.

I'm going to gives details for building a free blog at Wordpress.com and Blogger.com because they are by far the most popular and, in my opinion, the best. However, there are many other sites; perhaps another is more suited to your needs. These things are fairly universal so my advice below can be followed for others.

Wordpress.com.

For another ebook and program called, *How to Make, Market and Sell Ebooks All for Free*, I've used Wordpress.com to create a totally free blog site to give an example. It's online at http://ebooksuccess4free.wordpress.com. I regularly update the home page while the other pages remain static.

If you're just starting out with Wordpress.com for a blog, here are some basics to get you going. After signing up, you'll need to Register a blog. *Remember to do homework and follow the Google Keyword Tool instructions in the chapter on **Deciding on a Domain Name**.* Then enter a blog name of your choice and a blog title that should be like a headline. Click to enter and Login. You should be sent to a Dashboard for your page, like a command central. Near the middle of the Dashboard page is a button that says Change Theme. Click on that and browse hundreds of choices from Random, A to Z, to Popular themes. And you can always change the template later without losing your work.

After choosing a template, get started creating a blog, even a throw-away entry that you'll toss later just to get a feel for the process. As you blog along, click Update or Visit Site to save changes and check its appearance. From the editing area, it's always a good idea to place your cursor over the little icons for an explanation of what they do. You'll quickly become familiar with them and the whole process. For instance, when you're typing a blog post, if the area feels too small to work in there's an icon like a computer screen that says Toggle Fullscreen Mode and gives you a larger work space.

Blog posts also can be labeled with Categories and Post Tags. These will help dramatically with SEO purposes and others finding your blog entry. *Make sure to fill these categories and tags out with your short-tail keywords. Your blog titles and text will be the places to load up on long-tail keywords.*

It would take an entire book to completely tutor someone to use Wordpress (or any blogging venue), but fortunately there's an excellent support forum that has thorough answers to almost any question. If not, you can always ask a question and get tailored advice. Also do a Wordpress tutorial search on YouTube, and you'll have dozens of instructional videos to choose from.

Wordpress has very few cons, primarily that they don't allow Google AdSense or JavaScript (can be dangerous and used maliciously). Because they don't allow certain types of coding, it means some applications, like PayPal buttons, are a bit trickier to implement but there are always solutions in the support forums.

Blogger.com.

Blogger is the other biggie I like. It has been around since 1999 and was bought by Google in 2002. It's extremely popular, user-friendly, ad-free and since Blogger's owned by Google it's also perfect for signing up with AdSense, Google Affiliate Network and being listing in the Google directory. (Blogger calls categories "Labels," and they work the same as on Wordpress.) Blogger has tons of customizable template choices plus a great tutorial area and forum. Blogger is where I started my first blog, http://www.thebigbangauthor.com (I pay $10 per year to have the custom domain name), and I've been extremely happy with it.

Sign up with Blogger at https://www.blogger.com/. Click the Create A Blog link. Fill in the pertinent information and begin the journey. Then choose a template and get started.

Blogger also has an excellent support forum. Find them through the Help tab and either click on the Help Forum or the Video Tutorials. One of the best videos to watch at the onset will be the getting started video at http://www.youtube.com/BloggerHelp.

There are dozens of other blog venues which might be better for people with specific needs, and so here's a partial list:

http://www.livejournal.com/ - preferred by site owners who enjoy adding their own CSS (cascading style sheets).

http://www.blogster.com/ - catered for photos and video, also offers free image hosting.

Finally on blogging, remember to add short-tail keywords, labels, categories and/or tags wherever boxes present themselves to do so. These are general terms that describe the subjects of your post to help search engines and people to find your blog. You can also add your name to these boxes as that will help with your branding.

Learn to View Page Source

Page source, what's that? It's like the blueprints for a website, which is also the way the robot spiders see your site and blog. To better understand how this SEO stuff works, we need to see the website as the spiders do, at least a little. Now we're going to discuss a bit of HTML code language but not a lot, so don't worry if this is new.

The first thing to do is get comfortable viewing the page source of any webpage. This can be accomplished a few ways:

1. If using Windows, type and hold Ctrl U. For Mac users, Cmd U.

2. In your browser's upper tab options, click on View and scroll down to Page Source.

3. Put your cursor on empty space anywhere within a webpage (not on a link or image), Right Click and scroll down to View Page Source.

Now you're viewing the page source of any webpage, and that's what the spiders see. Like people, most websites have two main sections: the head and body. The start of the head section is designated by <head> and its end by </head>. The body section is done the same with <body> to start and </body> to end.

Much information is conveyed in both of these areas. What you normally see when visiting a webpage is primarily the body. The head areas are seen partly as titles above the browser or not at all as metadata for spiders and search engines. Here's a bit more about them and pieces you might see while viewing the HTML source of a common page:

<html> This signals the start of HTML code language.

<head> This is the beginning of the head or header information.

<title> This is the title above the browser bar. It doesn't show up on the page itself.

</title> End of the title area.

<meta name="Description" content="This is where the meta description goes, written in normal text and shows up under the listed URL in a Google search."/>

<meta name="Keywords" content="This is where the (optional) meta keywords go, each keyword or phrase separated by a comma."/>

</head> End of the head section.

<body> This is where the content of the webpage begins and is typically packed with more information than the head section.

</body> End of the body section.

</html> End of the HTML language.

We don't need to go into a massive HTML tutorial. For anyone wanting extras, there are always free online tips from a simple search, such as *how do I make text bold in HTML?* And the answer will be to use these tags, <b> and </b>, so that the word "example" with those tags around it, <b>example</b> will read on the page as **example**.

For now, let's return to Linda Marshall and her UFO project. After optimizing her metadata, the beginning parts of

Linda's website might look like this to someone (or something) viewing the page source:

```
<html>
<head>
<title>UFOs, Aliens and Area 51: Real UFO Sightings, Alien Abduction stories, Flying Saucer Photos by Linda Marshall.</title>
<meta name="Description" content="Find real UFO experiences, UFO sightings and photos, alien abductions. Linda Marshall is the expert in the ET field and Area 51. Read eyewitness accounts of flying saucers, UFOs and documentaries of real people having close encounters of the fourth kind."/>
<meta name="Keywords" content="UFO, aliens, area 51, UFO sighting, UFO video, alien abduction stories, flying saucer, Linda Marshall, alien photos, UFO photos, SETI, (and this could include several more but I'll let Linda do this optional homework)"/>
</head>
<body> <b>UFO</b> hunters, welcome! Here we have UFO video, photos, accounts from actual people in flying saucer rides and alien abduction stories... (the rest of Linda's webpage continues here with text, photos, video, links etc. Notice how her first keyword is also set to appear as bold text?)
</body>
</html>
```

That's a good chunk of the HTML code you'll want to understand for optimizing a website and blog. Now we'll look at each of these elements individually and how to make the most of them.

GOGFP Step #6. Get comfortable viewing page source and looking for elements that are related to SEO.

Optimize Page Titles

The title of your page is what visitors will see above their browser; it normally reads like a headline. It will also be the first line of a Google result from a search. Below the title will be the meta description, and below that will be the URL address. Here's an example from one of my sites if someone typed "The Little Universe" into a Google search:

Spiritual books by Jason Matthews, The Little Universe

Jason Matthews author of spiritual books, new age books, The Little Universe and Jim's Life. Enlightenment, healing by touch, meditation, awakening. *www.thelittleuniverse.com/*

In the above example, the title is *Spiritual books by Jason Matthews, The Little Universe*. It looks like this in the page source:

<title>Spiritual books by Jason Matthews, The Little Universe</title>

As you can see I have three of my most important keywords in this title field: spiritual books, the little universe and my name for branding. Also notice how Google highlights it and makes the title a clickable hyperlink to send a person to the website.

On many sites, each individual page can have individual titles. This strategy helps vary the titles according to what that unique page offers, meshing with other keywords. On another page of this same site, the title might be *Spiritual books by Jason Matthews, Jim's Life*, because that's the page for another novel yet I still want to brand myself and that subject. Or it could be *New Age books, Jim's Life by Jason Matthews*. Your individual pages might have far more different titles from page to page.

Here are some tips for maximizing the SEO factors of your title:

- Titles should be up to 66 characters (including spaces between words). That's how many characters Google will display in search results, so a longer title gets cut off.
- Titles need to be readable yet contain keywords, from most important to least.
- It should read like a Newspaper Headline with the First Letter of Main Keywords Capitalized.

Common title tags mistakes include:

- Having no title at all. It's amazing how many sites make this gross error (especially sites that haven't "made it big" yet).
- Each page having exactly the same title.
- Not reading like a headline. Keywords need to be in there but not totally stuffed.

Here are some titles you may recognize:

Facebook

Amazon.com: Online Shopping for Electronics, Apparel, Computers, Books, DVDs & more

ESPN: The Worldwide Leader In Sports

National and Local Weather Forecast, Hurricane, Radar and Report

CNN.com - Breaking News, U.S., World, Weather, Entertainment & Video News

Electronics, Cars, Fashion, Collectibles, Coupons and More Online Shopping | eBay

Twitter

Notice that Facebook and Twitter are doing pretty well without optimizing their title tags. Also see how common the symbol "&" is for "and" since title space is at a premium with 66 characters. It's true that Amazon and eBay don't care if their title tags get cut off in the search listings beyond 66 characters, as they care more about the browser's top title of their webpages containing all of the words they want. So while 66 characters are recommended, it won't hurt to have more.

I enjoy checking out famous page sources, so maybe you will too.

GOGFP Step #7. Optimize your HTML title <title> information for up to 66 characters with a few keywords from high to low priority that reads like a headline.

Metadata, Meta Description and (optional) Meta Keywords

This is very similar to optimizing the title, and there's more space to work with here. The main place to add them is to the Meta Description, and then the choice to insert Meta Keywords has been optional for a while.

Why? Google has changed their policy of old, and the other major search engines have followed suit. Google still cares deeply for the description content but not the keywords content. And since they don't list your Meta Keywords, there's not much need for them. However, Google and other search engines still read Meta Keywords, so why not add them anyway? The more I research this, the more my answer is *why the heck not?* Once you understand how to add them, it's very simple and then those terms are harmlessly listed. Perhaps there are hidden benefits that Google or others aren't being entirely transparent about. Admittedly, I could be dead wrong on this, but I'm adding Meta Keywords anyway. Consider it optional but possibly a helpful thing to do in the long run.

It's the Meta Description that is mandatory and included as the first few lines of descriptive text under your URL listing. For this reason, *Meta Descriptions are hugely important to both search engines and potential visitors.*

The HTML page source for our tutorial looks like this:

<meta name="Description" content="This is descriptive text that shows up on a search below the title tag and above the URL address. It usually gets cut off at 150 characters like th..." />

Google cuts off descriptions after 150 characters, so that's where the bulk of your message goes, if not all of it. Again, you can use more than 150 characters, but they won't show up. Here's another chance to write in a readable style yet packed with keywords, like a longer advertisement for viewers and spiders to see what your page has to offer.

GOGFP Step #8. Optimize your Meta Description to be up to 150 characters, with several keywords generally from high to low priority, and good for human readers to attract clicks.

The optional Meta Keywords is a spot to add (basically) all of your keywords. Consensus in the past was that up to 874 characters could be used, but it's probably safer to stay well less than that. I use around 250 to 300 characters and try not to have any one word repeat itself more than 4 or 5 times.

The HTML coding for the Meta Keywords looks like this (using Linda's example):

<meta name="Keywords" content="UFO, aliens, area 51, UFO sighting, UFO video, alien abduction stories, flying saucer, Linda Marshall, alien photos, UFO photos, SETI, (and this could include several more but I'll let Linda do that homework)" />

Now that we know the HTML coding, and that Meta Description matters a bunch and Meta Keywords perhaps not at all but still optional, the question is *how do we add them to your sites?*

Adding HTML Code to Your Sites

Depending on the type of site and method used to work within it, the need for editing HTML code will come into play differently. Many blogs are not really designed to manipulate keyword description, for example, and they have their own method of inserting titles. Other sites are easy to access the entire HTML coding and add the exact metadata you want.

If the blog site is with Wordpress.com, then it will accept a title and brief description, but there's no real way to add a meta description. Go through the Dashboard, choose Settings and General, the title and brief description (which can be like a meta description) should be added. When your blog comes up in a Google search, it will have the title highlighted and hyperlinked while the description will usually be the first lines of your most recently indexed post. Do not fear for the lack of metadata options; my Wordpress.com blog consistency has excellent SER (search engine ranking).

If your blog is with Blogger, there is an Edit HTML function. Just sign in and go to the Dashboard, then Design and the Edit HTML tab to access it. *Very important, copy and save the existing code in case anything goes wrong and you need to revert back to the original.* Then after the start of the head <head> area you can add your personalized meta description and keywords as in:

<meta name="Description" content="This is where the meta description goes, written in normal text and shows up under the listed URL in a Google search, although with a Blogger blog what will show is likely your last indexed post."/>

<meta name="Keywords" content="This is where the optional meta keywords go, each keyword or phrase separated by a comma."/>

Remember, you don't need a meta tag for the title because Blogger will already have a Title box that you filled out under Settings when you started the blog. That can always be changed too.

If you have a website with cPanel for accessing the inner workings, then the process is similar. Go through your File Manager and the Public_html/www Web Root area. There you can access each page like the home page, which should be listed as Index.html. Check that page then open the tab that says Edit Code. *Again copy and save the existing HTML code in case anything goes wrong and you need to reinsert it.* Then paste your meta description and keywords as explained above anywhere in the head section after <head> and before the end of the header </head>.

If you have FrontPage, Dreamweaver or basically any other HTML editor, it should have simple instructions for adding this to your webpage.

Also be sure your site has H1, or heading tags, early in the body section. This can be confusing *because the H1 header tag does not go in the <head> section*, but it goes in the <body> section. It is not the title <title> tag which appears above the browser but a heading tag and will appear like a heading (or title to keep it confusing) at the top of your page body. A H1 tag will make your text bigger, so that <h1>example</h> becomes example, but it is not meant to be a substitute for bold or larger font size. It alerts people and spiders to keywords. Most blog sites automatically fill this out with your title. You can do a simple view of the Page Source to see if there's an <h1> entry near the beginning of the <body> section. If not, and you can access your HTML editing, try adding a heading tag at the beginning of the body section like this:

<body>

<h1>Running Shoes to Fit Every Foot</h1>

You can also add a hyperlink to the home page (or any other page) by doing something like this:

<h1><a href="http://runningshoes.com/">Running Shoes to Fit Every Foot</a></h1>, which will result in a heading having a hyperlink to go to its home page.

You can also use other heading tags from H1 (largest size) down to H6 (smallest) to identify different sections within a page that require different titles and keywords.

GOGFP Step #9. Make sure your sites have the HTML code edited to include your title, meta description and (optional) keywords. Also add an H1 title tag if it's not there already. Then check the Page Source to make sure they are all in.

Page Body Keywords

Now it's time to optimize the text within each page, the words in the body <body> section. While this is the place to really get out keywords, both short and long-tail, it's also a place to beware of keyword stuffing.

The basic rule of thumb is to get your keywords out there, both short and long-tail, while keeping it pleasant to read.

There are several factors to consider including: Density, Frequency, Prominence and Proximity.

Density is the percentage of times a keyword or phrase appears compared to all of the other words on the page combined. While Google has said that they no longer purposely factor Density into the algorithm, the basic rule of thumb is to keep your keywords repeating themselves while the text is still pleasant to read. Having a keyword density of 10%, or every tenth word being that same repeating keyword, is considered Black Hat and very risky. A safer ratio is 3% to 8%.

Frequency is similar to Density. It's the number of times a keyword is repeated, and the same rule of pleasant reading should apply. While it's important to repeat you main keywords a few times throughout the page body, it can also look like spam if it seems exaggerated or doesn't read well.

Google won't give any official numbers, but consensus seems to be that anything more than four or five times repeating a keyword is taking a Black Hat risk.

Prominence is how close to the beginning of the content your main keywords appear. These keywords should come up as soon as possible, definitely within the first sentence. I also like to use **bold** text for this first appearance and again before the end of the page. For an example from my website that teaches others to sell ebooks, the text might begin as such; *If you want to **sell ebooks**, you're at the right place. This site is an example for methods to accomplish that. Everything here is 100% free...*

Proximity is how close individual keywords are to each other. Obviously, the closer they are, the more relationship they appear to have. Closer is better. For example, if two of your keywords are "Detroit area" and "faux finish painting," then which of the following would have better proximity? "For greater Detroit area faux finish painting, we're the pros to call," or "For faux finish painting in the greater Detroit area, we're the pros to call"? The first example has better proximity (or closeness) for those keywords.

GOGFP Step #10. Use short and long-tail keywords in the text of the page body while paying attention to Density, Frequency, Prominence and Proximity. You can also use bold text to emphasize Prominence.

Submit URL Directly to Google and Others

Even though your site will be indexed eventually even if you do nothing, it's a good idea to submit the site manually to Google. It's smart to do it elsewhere too, so I have a list of places ready to help with their search engines. However, it is not necessary or recommended to submit your site to hundreds or thousands of search engines. Stick with the big outfits and you'll be fine.

As to regularity, it's not really important to update a submission after making changes to a site. Google even reports; *only the top-level page from a host is necessary; you do not need to submit each individual page. Our crawler, Googlebot, will be able to find the rest. Google updates its index on a regular basis, so updated or outdated link submissions are not necessary. Dead links will 'fade out' of our index on our next crawl when we update our entire index.* However, you may feel better doing it after major updates, and there's probably no harm in repeat submissions. It will still take time for your URL to show up in a search with Google or any other engine even after you've submitted it correctly. It might take as little as a few days or as long as a few weeks. Unfortunately this is out of your control so be patient if it doesn't appear as soon as you'd prefer. Remember the way to check if your site has been indexed is to type the exact URL address, as in http://example.com into a search. If your listing appears on top with the *updated Page Source info,* then it has been indexed. If not, give it a week or two to go through.

Here's the list of the best free places to add your URL for their directories:

https://www.google.com/webmasters/tools/submit-url - Submit your sites directly to Google.

http://www.bing.com/toolbox/submit-site-url - Submit your sites to Bing, which has merged with Yahoo Site Explorer.

http://www.scrubtheweb.com/ - A great place to submit your sites to 10 major search engines at once. This outfit also evaluates the effectiveness of your SEO strategies and provides recommendations such as "the Title should be less than 60 characters," though that number is not consistent with Google's cut off point of 66. Scrub The Web has been around since 1996 and has both free and paid services for helping anyone maximize their SEO performance. If you do use them to submit to multiple search engines, remember to un-check the box for Google since there is no need to resubmit with them.

DMOZ.org - This is a human-powered directory run by volunteers. They call it an Open Directory Project and attempt to recognize the best sites in content. The DMOZ is selective and may take several weeks to approve and index a site while also rejecting many submissions. Because their procedure is more complicated and run by people, Google and other search engines take notice and appreciate sites indexed with DMOZ. There are other human-powered directories, but they are largely paid services so I'm not listing them here. They can easily be found with a search for submitting to directories.

Blog Catalog - http://www.blogcatalog.com/ - a premiere social blog directory for those looking to promote your own blog, find blogs on various topics, or connect with other bloggers. There are also many other blog directories that can be found with a search, but I like this one and it's free.

GOGFP Step #11. Freely submit your URL directly to Google. You should also do Bing, DMOZ and ScrubTheWeb while considering other places optional.

Google Webmaster Tools

Use the Google Webmaster Tools and Meta Tags or HTML Code to verify your sites. I'll give a few examples at different locations, but the process is basically this; *Google wants you to upload a file or code to your website to immediately verify that you are the site owner.*

Remember back when you may have created a blog with Wordpress, they should have provided these links to verify it with the big three search engines here - http://en.support.wordpress.com/webmaster-tools/. This procedure works for verifying with Google and Bing search engines by adding Meta Tags or HTML code that will be crawled and identified. Help with this can also be found through the Dashboard of your Wordpress blog, *and this also works for any website.* If you scroll down the left side you'll eventually find a tab that says Tools. Click on it and scroll down to the Webmaster Verification Tools. There you will see the boxes that go with the Meta Tags you'll be asked to input by using the link above to visit the big search engines. And this will help too - http://en.support.wordpress.com/search-engines/. The Wordpress tutorial is here - http://en.support.wordpress.com/webmaster-tools/.

For Wordpress.com and Yola.com I chose the Meta Tag Verification and followed their tutorials as these places make it very easy to insert. The Yola tutorial is here - http://www.yola.com/tutorials/article/Tutorial-Google-Webmaster-1285944435809/Promotion,-SEO,-Traffic-and-Advertising, and since Blogger is owned by Google that help is here - http://www.google.com/support/webmasters/.

With Webs.com, they only allow Meta Tags for Premium or paid members, so the free site people will use the HTML Code option, which is similar for anyone who can add a bit of HTML coding within the homepage of a website. Here the Google Verification process is a tiny bit more involved but you can do it.

- Once you get to the Google Verification site - https://www.google.com/webmasters/tools/home?hl=en, click the Add a Site button and enter the URL of your website including the prefix as in example.webs.com. It will ask if you want to verify with a Meta Tag or an HTML file.

- For Webs.com I chose the HTML file, which it then created for me and asked me to Download the HTML file. When you download it, Open it then Save it by choosing Save Page As a Web Page HTML file on your desktop or in a folder.

- Then I returned to Webs.com where I Single File Uploaded it to my File Manager (Browse your Desktop or folder for that Google file and make sure the entire suffix looks exactly the same as the link Google shows).

- Then I went to Edit my Homepage, scrolled to the bottom and typed in "Google" (any letters will do). I clicked to highlight the word "Google," then went to Link to Insert a Link, from My Files and chose the Google HTML file and Insert.

- Then I published the page and returned to Site Manager.

- Once this was done, I returned to the Google Verify page, where it asked me to Confirm a successful upload by visiting a site it highlighted. (This should take you to a blank webpage with "Google" and many letters/numbers in the upper left corner. It should result in exactly the same thing if you click on your Home Page file link you just created over the word "Google." Test them in windows side by side to see if they're **exactly** the same; if they're not, try the process again.)

- Once I had visited the site in another window, I returned and clicked the Verify button and it worked instantly. I know this sounds complex, but if I can do it so can you.

GOGFP Step #12. Verify your sites directly with Google. Others are optional.

Adding and Submitting a Sitemap

Even though Google claims only the home page is necessary to submit, the consensus among SEO experts is that submitting a sitemap can only benefit in SER. A sitemap will immediately alert search engines of every page on your site approved for them to crawl.

Some webhosts make it very easy to submit a sitemap. With places like Yola and Wordpress, if you complete the verification process with Google, then Submitting a Sitemap is a simple extra step and something they recommend. Google says; *sitemaps are a way to tell Google about pages on your site we might not otherwise discover. In its simplest terms, a XML Sitemap—usually called Sitemap, with a capital S—is a list of the pages on your website. Creating and submitting a Sitemap helps make sure that Google knows about all the pages on your site, including URLs that may not be discoverable by Google's normal crawling process.*

This can be as easy as clicking on the Submit a Sitemap button and adding the suffix, /sitemap.xml to your URL as in http://example.com/sitemap.xml. Try it with your site and see if it works first. If not, there's a simple program for it and things may change so check back. However, you can also verify each page individually if you want to be certain Google knows more than just your homepage. *The HTML file is exactly the same for any page or any site that you create,* so just load the

HTML file onto a page and verify it with Google. Once you understand the process it takes very little time.

There are also programs that freely create sitemaps for you. XML-sitemaps is one I recommend - http://www.xml-sitemaps.com. Simply follow the prompts to enter the URL domain name, download the sitemap file it creates, then upload that file into the file manager area of your website. If that's done correctly, the next step is to go to Google Webmaster Tools, click on the site and follow the prompts to Submit a Sitemap. It usually takes a few hours to verify the sitemap, which will show a green checkmark under the Status.

It's also wise to help human visitors find each webpage. For instance, some navigation bars at the top of the page are a relative pain to scroll back up in order to click on the next page. (People are lazy, I know.) It's helpful to add a navigation menu at the bottom of each page that are clickable hyperlinks to send a visitor anywhere within the site. For example, having a bottom line that reads Home - About Us - Products - Contact - Links, and linking for the appropriate page will help both human visitors and spiders navigate your website.

GOGFP Step #13. Submit a sitemap to Google, and optimize the ease with which visitors navigate your webpages.

Google Analytics, Alerts
and Other Programs

Google has many free programs that are extremely helpful. There are a few I consider to be mandatory. Here's a partial list:

Google Analytics - http://www.google.com/analytics/
Google Analytics is the enterprise-class web analytics solution that gives you rich insights into your website traffic and marketing effectiveness. Powerful, flexible and easy-to-use features now let you see and analyze your traffic data in an entirely new way. With Google Analytics, you're more prepared to write better-targeted ads, strengthen your marketing initiatives and create higher converting websites.

The statistics are quite in-depth, including categories like pages/visit, bounce rate (when visitors left after just seeing your landing page) and average time at site. It will take a while to get comfortable with their reports so it's smart to check into it regularly and click on different features.

Google Alerts - http://www.google.com/alerts/
This is an incredibly helpful tool for online marketing. Think of it like a little bird that notifies you of any information pertaining to your subjects of interest. I use them for my book titles, my name and also for things like self-

publishing and selling ebooks. For those who aren't familiar with Google Alerts, this is how the company describes them;

Google Alerts are email updates of the latest relevant Google results (web, news, etc.) based on your choice of query or topic. Some handy uses of Google Alerts include:

-monitoring a developing news story
-keeping current on a competitor or industry
-getting the latest on a celebrity or event
-keeping tabs on your favorite sports teams

I use them to help with marketing efforts and finding blogs of similar subject matter. For example, I get alerts each day about anything on the subject of selling ebooks. I can then click on those links and read the current articles and blogs. Usually there will be a comment box where I can leave a helpful comment and include a small blurb about my ebook and a link. As long as I'm not blatantly spamming an advertisement, it's really easy to get my message and URL links out there for others to click on.

To get started, visit the site and fill out the form with your search terms and information. Google will email you with any web content that appears. Then visit those articles and blog posts. If there's a comment box, leave a thoughtful reply and insert your URL which will be a clickable part of your name next to your comment. You can often type in a URL in the comment area itself that will become hyperlinked. I recommend leaving at least two or three comments per day so your potential for new visitors will increase dramatically over the following weeks and months.

Google   Webmaster   Tools   -
https://www.google.com/webmasters/tools/home/

We've already spoken about this as a place to directly submit a website and have it verified by Google. You can also submit your sitemap here.

Google Trends - http://www.google.com/trends/
This feature helps compare search volume patterns across specific regions, categories, time frames and properties.

Google Maps - http://maps.google.com/
If the physical location is important for your business, then this is a great place to add a listing.

Other free and useful Google programs:
AdSense - https://www.google.com/adsense - for those wanting to advertise on their sites and make a little extra money.
Groups - http://groups.google.com - social networking and more.
Videos - http://video.google.com - for finding videos.
Video Sitemap - https://developers.google.com/webmasters/videosearch/ - for creating sitemap content that helps spiders see the relevant keywords of your videos. (We'll talk about this more later.)
Images - http://images.google.com - an enormous collection of online images.
GOGFP Step #14. Use every free Google program that is related to your projects, especially Analytics, Alerts and Webmaster Tools.

Backlinks, PageRank and Link Building

The main element of online success is effectively driving traffic to your website. If you had no problems with that, SEO knowledge wouldn't be needed. However, most people must work to attract visitors, and one of the most common ways is by leaving the URL link of your website at many locations. People can read a blurb about the site, click on the link and come for a visit. You probably do this every time you're surfing online, often without realizing it.

Backlinks, link building and even link baiting are terms that describe the simple act of leaving your URL hyperlinks at other locations designed to get visitors to click and come to your site. The more links a site has pointing to it, the more likely the site is an authority on its subject in the eyes of Google. In addition to the number of sites pointing to yours, the quality of those sites also matters, as in *higher quality sites that point to yours are worth more than lower quality sites*. Quality of the site is also referred to as PageRank.

This is how Google describes PageRank;
PageRank reflects our view of the importance of web pages by considering more than 500 million variables and 2 billion terms. (Thankfully they don't list them.) *Pages that we believe are important pages receive a higher PageRank and are more likely to appear at the top of the search results.*

PageRank also considers the importance of each page that casts a vote, as votes from some pages are considered to have greater value, thus giving the linked page greater value. We have always taken a pragmatic approach to help improve search quality and create useful products, and our technology uses the collective intelligence of the web to determine a page's importance.

Initially you will have more control improving the quantity of incoming links. Over time, with good content, the quality of inbound links will improve by itself.

For those getting started, focus on quantity. The more links connected to your blog and website, the better. In time, the quality will improve if you have good content because others will want to add a link to your site. The general rule of thumb is this; *do what you can to get your URL links onto many other sites.*

Search engines record each time someone clicks a link that goes to one of your pages, and over time they start to recognize you're becoming more popular. Make it a habit to spread your links out to anywhere and everywhere possible, especially on all of the social media sites and places you visit as well as in the articles that you'll write (which we'll cover soon in the Social Media and PR Public Relations chapters). As I'll discuss, *you can also leave comments on other people's blogs,* which is a great way to add input and leave your URL as most blogs that take comments will have a box for URLs. Leaving comments on blogs for subjects that interest you is an excellent way to spread your URLs around.

Now, an obvious tip is to click on those links back to your blog and website. Number one, it's smart to make sure the links work, and secondly those clicks will register with the search engines. Whenever I visit a major site that has one of my links, I'll click on it just to remind Google of the connection to my site.

GOGFP Step #15. Always leave your URL in a hyperlinked method whenever and wherever you can to continually plant backlinks like Johnny Appleseed.

Remember the story of Johnny Appleseed, the American pioneer who roamed the countryside planting apple seeds? This account might be fictionalized, but it's a great metaphor for how you should approach a link building campaign. Every day, make it a habit to put your URL link to at least three separate places. By the end of the year you'll have over a thousand links pointing to your website in addition to the other people who start recommending your site.

Here's a quick success story on this. I made a simple comment at a popular blog discussing how much I liked a free webhost and used it for designing a website. I left my URL in the comment for others to check and see how a total beginner faired at building his first website. In a year's time over 400 visitors came to my site from that single link. Of course, this is a great example and most links generate fewer visitors, but the concept is powerful. It's not a stretch to generate many thousands of yearly visitors by simply leaving your URL at a few websites everyday like a Johnny Appleseed character.

How and where should you do this?

In many locations, like other people's blogs, there will be boxes for your name, email and URL to be filled out before making a comment. Those are the really easy places. They are perfectly designed to turn your name into a hyperlink for your site once the comment is posted and/or approved. Always make sure to leave the URL as in http://yourdomainname.com. Also leave a thoughtful comment that doesn't sound like spam *because this is one of those areas that can be a fine line between White Hat and Black Hat SEO.*

Within some comment boxes, you can also use HTML coding. It will usually explain underneath the comment box if you can or not. If it's allowed, you might want to hyperlink a set of words to go directly to your website. For instance, let's say your website is for marriage counseling, and you want to leave the following line of text on a blog about spouses that have grown apart;

Please don't give up. Our counselors can help you mend any relationship worth saving.

It would be great to add some HTML coding to make that comment stand out and also have a backlink to the website. You could write this instead (if the comment box takes HTML);

Please don't give up. Our counselors can help you <a href=http://www.goodtherapy.org/>mend any relationship</a> worth saving.

If you did that, the comment would be hyperlinked to the website and read like this;

Please don't give up. Our counselors can help you mend any relationship worth saving.

Now that would be a helpful comment which adds to the discussion and creates a free advertisement to your marriagecounselors.com website. It's one of those win-win situations that also helps greatly with SEO.

We're going to discuss backlinks throughout the Social Media and Public Relations chapters.

Alternative Text and Title Attributes
for Images

Here's an update from Google;

Some of you have asked about the difference between the "alt" and "title" attributes. According to the W3C recommendations, the "alt" attribute specifies an alternate text for user agents that cannot display images, forms or applets. The "title" attribute is a bit different: it "offers advisory information about the element for which it is set." As the Googlebot does not see the images directly, we generally concentrate on the information provided in the "alt" attribute. Feel free to supplement the "alt" attribute with "title" and other attributes if they provide value to your users!

Google is saying that the alternative (alt) text is far more important than the title attributes but both can still be done. Okay, what are we talking about?

Spiders can't see pictures on a screen like most humans do. Some visually impaired people, browsers or computers can't either. Alternative text (also called alt text, alt attributes or associated text) for images is helpful with this, as in wording that accompanies a picture for clarifying what it's about. The alt text is seen by the spiders as important words on the page since pictures usually are very descriptive of the content. This text is a part of the HTML coding and only seen normally with a View of Page Source or right click, View Image Info.

For example, on a webpage with a photo of a baseball player hitting a game-winning home run, the written article is likely about the game, the player and the final result. The picture of the home run isn't seen by Googlebots or visually impaired people, but an alternative text description of "Baseball player Mike Philips hits game winning home-run" will explain that, thus contributing to keyword credit for the article's URL and the image. It will also get the photo listed in Google Image searches over time for anyone looking for pictures of Mike Philips, game-winning home runs or baseball players. The picture would likely come up soon for a "Mike Philips" search, not so soon for a "game-winning home run" search and probably thousands to millions of images later for a "baseball player" search.

(Note—just for fun go to Google Images and search for your name to see any online photos that have been associated with you via alternative text or other means.)

A normally inserted picture may appear to the spiders like this in HTML code (as it would with a view of the page source):

<img src="http://ecx.images-18,34_OU01_.jpg" />

The above fictional example might be a fantastic picture but would mean nothing to spiders or anyone else who can't properly see the image.

An SEO preferred version with alternative text including a title attribute would be this:

<img src="http://ecx.images-18,34_OU01_.jpg" alt="UFO expert Linda Marshall, Roswell New Mexico"

title="UFO expert Linda Marshall doing alien research in Roswell, New Mexico" />

Now the SEO spiders and visually impaired can get more info about the photo. Also notice that there is often redundancy between the alt text and the title attribute which is probably why Google has announced they really just focus on the alt text.

You can easily check if an image has alternative text associated with it by either viewing the page source or viewing the image info. Right click on a picture within a webpage and scroll down to View Image Info. If the Associated Text has relevant information to the picture, then that will help with SEO purposes for both the article's URL and the photo itself. It will also help with user experience, which is what Google is focused on.

Some things to remember when adding alt text:

- Alt text should describe what the image is while also reading well to a visually impaired person.
- For active images, e.g. containing a hyperlink, the alt text should describe what it will do.
- If the image itself is simply text, then the alt text should be the same.

Here's another example of adding alt text to enhance the spider and user experience. The below picture is one of my beloved, passed dog, Shep.

The actual text for the image which the spiders would see looks something like this: <img src="http://1.bp.blogspot.com/_vvumW_9VCWg/TRJA7_t qOQI/AAAAAAAACJs/sGRmkT8vYhE/s320/Shep+Face. jpg" but that doesn't mean much to spiders or the visually impaired.

If I add alt text to the image, it might now look something like this: <img src="http://1.bp.blogspot.com/_vvumW_9VCWg/TRJA7_t qOQI/AAAAAAAACJs/sGRmkT8vYhE/s320/Shep+Face. jpg" alt="Shep and Jason Matthews in Reno Nevada" which would tell the spiders and others that this image is of Shep and me taken in Reno. (True, I'm not a big part of the picture (nor is Reno) but I am there, and this thing still helps with branding for both Shep and me.)

Now a Google Image search for "Shep and Jason Matthews" should contain this picture.

GOGFP Step #16. Always use alternative text (alt text) to accompany your images. Consider title attributes optional.

Video and Video SEO

Since its creation a little over a hundred years ago, video has been the supreme global medium. From "moving pictures" to television to "viral video," the potential uses are impressive. Video should be wisely incorporated with any SEO strategy as it will likely become ever bigger in search results.

However, don't be fooled by some recommendations that say video is mandatory for SEO. I believe great results can be had without it, and simultaneously video can help tremendously if done right. The reason I say that is because if you do a current Google search, often the front page does not have any video included. Sure, there are plenty of exceptions, but do some testing and you'll see that it's true as of September 2014.

It's also true that Google has a policy of "blended search" results which include video, images, news features, maps and more. Sometimes video results do show up on the first page, and I admit to a tendency to click on the video options often. Perhaps you do too. Also notice most of the videos are from YouTube, which happens to be owned by Google. Some of the videos are from privately owned websites or from other video venues.

It's important to recognize both the potential of video and the different methods of uploading. In general you have two choices: upload to a venue warehouse like YouTube or upload to your own website.

Google says; *Video content is one of the most popular rich media formats in the world. For example, Google's video site video.google.com is the largest video search property on the Web. One of the best ways to improve your site's appearance in video search results is to make sure that Google knows about all your rich video content. When you submit a Sitemap to Google that includes video information in a supported format, we will make the included video URLs searchable on Google Video. When a user finds your video through Google, they will be linked to your hosted environments for the full playback...*

...You can create a separate Sitemap listing your video content, or you can add information about your video content to an existing Sitemap—whichever is more convenient for you.

The Google video extension of the Sitemap protocol enables you to give Google descriptive information—such as a video's title, description, duration, etc.—that makes it easier for users to find a particular piece of content...

...You can create a Sitemap based on the Sitemap protocol, or you can use an existing mRSS feed as a Sitemap, or both.

Your Sitemap will need to include the following minimum information for each video: title, description, playpage URL, thumbnail URL and the raw video URL or URL to Flash video player. Without these five pieces of information, Google cannot surface your videos in our results.

Once you've created your Sitemap, you can submit it using Webmaster Tools. More information about adding video information to a Sitemap.

Notice how Google discusses the **need to submit a video sitemap?** Just because you may have an embedded YouTube (or other source) video playing on a website, that doesn't mean the robot spiders can see the video and know what it's about. This is something we'll discuss in just a moment, but first a few words on video in general.

Obviously it makes sense to create videos on any subject and share them at popular sites. People see the video and can then investigate more of what you have to offer. It's free for everyone and creates good business. Besides YouTube, there are several sites where you may want to upload video, and this is growing all the time. Here's a partial list to consider:

YouTube - the world's largest video sharing community and second largest search engine! (Now that Google owns YouTube, they no longer offer uploading of video directly to Google but they still search and list the category thoroughly.)

Yahoo Video - Yahoo would love to see this take a chunk out of YouTube.

Vimeo - community of video sharing people.

MetaCafe - primarily entertainment, selectively chosen videos.

DailyMotion - online videos, music and movies.

TubeMogul - a distribution service (both free and paid options) that spreads your uploads to everywhere you have accounts. It's a huge time-saver for active video producers.

CNN - upload newsworthy video through their iReport program.

Steps to take:

1. Make a video. We all have different skills and money available for this. If you're like me, you might be willing to do an amateur production since you believe the message is ultimately more important than the presentation. You'll still want to follow the rule that *content is king* and produce the

best video you can, even if you're working alone on a budget of zero dollars. I find videos that are short, around 1 to 4 minutes, get watched more than longer videos.

2. Rename the video file something along the lines of your best relevant keywords, both short and long-tail. It will not help to have a video that is titled by default something like 125-0356.mov, when it could be saved as something like *How to Deep Fry a Turkey.*

3. Upload a video to YouTube. There are many good and a few not so good reasons to upload with YouTube. The positives are that it's the world's largest video service and owned by Google. On Google searches, the top videos listed are primarily from YouTube regardless of the subject. Unfortunately, YouTube doesn't accommodate hyperlinks within videos nor in the comment boxes below. They do allow for a URL to be *hyperlinked in the description area* for the video. Besides leaving a link there, the URL can be added to the video itself as a caption, but that requires users to retype it so the domain name should be clear and on-screen long enough to notice. The other drawback is that the search results are leading a user to YouTube and not directly to your website, which would be better for SEO.

At YouTube (or any similar service), when you input the terms for the title, description and tags, remember to maximize each of these for the relevant keywords that the video is for. Also notice that even though the description area barely shows to the human visitors during playback, it is completely read by Googlebot spiders, so don't skimp on the description. *Consider the description box a moment for sales copy and load up on all of your relevant keywords.*

4. Upload a video to anywhere else you'd like, including the sites listed above or others.

5. Upload video directly to your own website as a video file, then put it on a page. This isn't going to happen with many free blogging platforms, but if you can access the file manager for uploading files (including video), then it should work. Depending on your operating system, follow their prompts to upload video files and place them on webpages. Then continue to the next step.

6. Submit a video sitemap to Google. Many people think just because they have a webpage indexed that contains video, that the video itself is also read and indexed. Not true. *Google spiders must have a video sitemap to read the title, description and tags for videos.* This page has a Google tutorial example for what an example video Sitemap page looks like - http://www.google.com/support/webmasters/bin/answer.py?hl=en&answer=80472.

A Video Sitemap is really just a text file with video specific tags in it. In its smallest form it would be a tag that links to the landing page for the video as in this Google example:

<urlset xmlns="http://www.sitemaps.org/schemas/sitemap/0.9"

   xmlns:video="http://www.google.com/schemas/sitemap-video/1.1">

   <url>

   <loc>http://www.example.com/videos/some_video_landing_page.html</loc>

   <video:video>

   <video:thumbnail_loc>http://www.example.com/thumbs/123.jpg</video:thumbnail_loc>

```
<video:title>Grilling steaks for summer</video:title>
<video:description>Alkis shows you how to get perfectly
done steaks every time</video:description>
<video:content_loc>http://www.example.com/video123
.flv</video:content_loc>
<video:player_loc                    allow_embed="yes"
autoplay="ap=1">
http://www.example.com/videoplayer.swf?video=123</
video:player_loc>
<video:duration>600</video:duration>
<video:expiration_date>2009-11-
05T19:20:30+08:00</video:expiration_date>
<video:rating>4.2</video:rating>
<video:view_count>12345</video:view_count>
<video:publication_date>2007-11-
05T19:20:30+08:00</video:publication_date>
<video:tag>steak</video:tag>
<video:tag>meat</video:tag>
<video:tag>summer</video:tag>
<video:category>Grilling</video:category>
<video:family_friendly>yes</video:family_friendly>
<video:restriction    relationship="allow">IE   GB   US
CA</video:restriction>
<video:gallery_loc                    title="Cooking
Videos">http://cooking.example.com</video:gallery_loc>
<video:price currency="EUR">1.99</video:price>
<video:requires_subscription>yes</video:requires_subsc
ription>
<video:uploader
info="http://www.example.com/users/grillymcgrillerson">
GrillyMcGrillerson
```

```
</video:uploader>
</video:video>
</url>
</urlset>
```

In the above example, you can substitute your own entries for the required parts: <loc>, <video:video>, <video:thumbnail_loc>, <video:title> and <video:description>. Either <video:content_loc> or <video:player_loc> is also required. All other attributes are optional but some are strongly recommended.

Once you've replaced the data for that example and uploaded the information to your file manager along with a sitemap for the page and/or entire site, then you can return to Webmaster Tools and submit your video sitemap. It's true that this is currently one of the more complicated things to do in this entire SEO field. I've personally had difficulty with this and hope Google makes it easier in the upcoming months for the average person to accomplish video sitemaps, especially since the field is growing in importance.

GOGFP Step #17. Submit video sitemaps directly to Google to enable direct links to your URL from video search results.

Social Media

I'd like to discuss social media and the concept of building an overall online platform to assist SEO efforts. *Your online platform can be thought of as your internet presence,* and it's vital for successfully marketing a website and services or products. A great way to solidify a foundation for online platform and internet presence is by establishing a social media network in several venues like Facebook, Twitter, **Google Plus,** Yahoo, YouTube, etc. Social media is an absolute must because it not only enables you to keep in touch with friends and family, *but it also enables multiple ways to connect with absolute strangers and for absolute strangers to have multiple ways to connect with you.* You must reach out to strangers from all over the world and enable portals for them to connect with you. When a perfect stranger contacts you from Botswana or Sri Lanka, it will probably make your day.

I'm going to list several social media sites that I consider mandatory, but this category is truly *the more the better.* Keep in mind; just because you have 5 or more accounts on social media sites doesn't mean you have to be active there on a daily basis. All you need is your presence there and links to your website/blog. Of course if you are active at some of these places it helps a lot, but it's not mandatory.

Here are several social media sites that are a must have:

Google Plus.

This may be seen as Google + or Google +1 or simply G+.

In my opinion, *Google Plus takes the best aspects of Facebook, Twitter and LinkedIn while eliminating the worst.* (However, Facebook made broad scale changes to its platform as a result of G+, so don't be surprised to see all of the venues becoming more alike in time.) Presently, Google Plus has a design that can be your one-stop for all things social media. Like Facebook, you can stream wall posts of what's happening or share comments and include video, links, photos, chat, etc. Unlike the old Facebook, you can create different "circles" that these posts go out to (though Facebook has made changes to accommodate this ability; it's just more time consuming to sort out for users who already have hundreds of FB friends). G+ circles can be composed of family, friends, work colleagues, the bowling league, sexy lingerie club… whatever kind of circle you want to create. To me, this is a huge difference over the original Facebook as you can easily select what others do or don't see with updates and wall posts. As I said, FB made changes after Google Plus came out, but it's a hassle to change the status of friends when you have several hundred.

The G+ program will also recommend people to add and you can easily choose the circles to place them, which is a great way for them to discover you as well.

Like Twitter, anyone can add you to their circle to follow, and you can add anyone to yours. Unlike Twitter, you can identify who you want to see what, and you can do many things their platform doesn't support.

The search bar at the top allows you to search Google Plus for content of interest. You can type in things like recipes, books, dog-walkers in Los Angeles or anything.

Hangouts allows group video chat with multiple people, another very cool feature. You can have meetings using hangouts with people from all over the world.

Because this social media site *does everything the other ones do and then some,* it feels like a must for anyone who wants the best of social media.

There are plenty of great tutorials on how to use Google Plus including these:

http://www.readwriteweb.com/archives/how_to_start_with_google_plus.php - article tutorial

http://www.stateofsearch.com/how-to-use-google-a-quick-guide-and-thoughts-on-google-plus/ - article tutorial

http://www.youtube.com/watch?v=5TDMObxEtEY&feature=related - video tutorial

You can also find badges by searching the term, *Google Plus Badges.* Here's one place I found that creates a nice photo ID for a badge - http://turhan.me/+me/. (You'll need to add the URL hyperlink of your Google Plus personal profile page when you insert it on a website or blog.)

My personal strategy is reserving Google Plus for business-networking, while I use Facebook for all my friends and family, although I also use FB for my group page. Group pages for businesses, products, artists or other categories can also be made at G+ by clicking the Create button in the Pages section currently listed in the More tab on the left side.

Facebook.com.

Recently Facebook has passed Google for daily users. This media mega-giant has over 1 billion users, 50% of which log in every single day. That's amazing, 500 million users each day! The average user has 130 friends, is a member of 13 groups and spends nearly an hour a day on the site. 70% of users live outside the US, and Facebook is translated into 70 different languages. You can access it from mobile devices, and the people that do so are reportedly twice as active on the site. Needless to say, Facebook is the grand champion. *If you're not on Facebook, you should get on it right away. And if you are on it, you want to maximize your ability to make connections.*

So either start a Facebook account or make the most of the one you have. Upload photos and/or video of yourself. Make friends with as many people as you're comfortable doing. Comment on other people's photos and walls frequently which will leave a lasting image of your presence. Manage your settings so that you get the email notifications you want. (That's all handled through your Account Tab in your Account Settings under the Notifications list.)

You should also join multiple groups on Facebook that have to do with your subjects of interest. Groups are designated by the little icon of two heads next to each other. Just click on it and search for groups. When you find ones that you like, post messages on their group wall as long as the *content is open for public* and tell them about your websites with the URL hyperlink. You can even create your own groups. Make connections and be interesting because people prefer that.

(An important reminder here; whenever posting anywhere keep your messages interesting and fun without looking like a spammer. *Try to add quality more than quantity.*

Keep posting regularly on the discussion boards, but alter them on each board so you don't get into trouble with Facebook. They have guidelines against Black Hat spamming the exact same message in a cut and paste fashion to multiple boards and members.)

If you haven't done so already, creating a Facebook Profile Badge, Fan Page and Group Page or Page Badge are excellent ways to link Facebook users to your website and to have HTML widgets that link back to your Facebook pages. Facebook has tutorials on making the widgets, and then placing them on your site is a simple HTML insert.

Twitter.com.

Some people have amazing results with Twitter although, for me, it's not as important as Facebook or Google Plus. Yet it's a must-have for social media. You need a Twitter account because there are exciting possibilities that exist on Twitter. You start "tweeting" regularly with things of interest and links to great articles, and people will find and follow you. It also helps to follow people who share things or deal with subjects that interest you, and these things can be "retweeted." What you'll learn on Twitter is you can write up to 140 characters and eventually connect with a lot of people. I'm not super active there, but I do have an application called Tweetdeck, which allows me to use this service even better. You can download Tweetdeck at http://www.tweetdeck.com/ or alternatives, which basically make Twitter a little easier to use and with more options.

How does someone use Twitter to create an audience and network? Keep it interesting. Share certain anecdotes or jokes or newsworthy stuff with links as you come across them. And yes, you can tweet about your website or blog but not constantly. That would get annoying to your followers, who might "unfollow" you.

The neat thing about Twitter is the fact that you might tweet a message others find interesting, and they might "retweet" (RT) it and so on until it gets seen by many thousands of people. I once did a blog entry on the uses for industrial hemp and made a tweet about it. One person who followed me "retweeted" it and the link to my blog site. She a large following, some of whom saw my tweet and visited my blog, which received far more visitors that day than usual.

These days many people have 50,000 or 100,000 followers or even more. I have far fewer but they're almost entirely writers and readers. You can either go for the big numbers or go for a relevant crowd to follow and follow back.

Use the @ **symbol** plus a person's Twitter name to include others in your tweets or make sure they get notified, especially in hopes of having them retweet.

You can also use *hash-tags* to help specify a message and gain relevant followers faster. Hash-tags are a way of searching within the billions of tweets for topic specific posts. It's simply the number symbol or pound sign (#) with a search term, like #SuperBowl or #Friday or even #elephant. To see if a search term is already being used, just type it in the Twitter search box at the top of the page and see how many results come up. Play around with closely related examples, like #fiction and #novel, to see which ones are more commonly used.

The same method can be used to find people with similar interests. Try hash tag terms for current events like this fictional example, #RenoFire. You can also play around with the terms in the Trends section on the home page.

There are many services designed to help increase your followers quickly. I don't use them since I prefer the organic method over time, but here are two:

http://www.tweetadder.com/

http://wefollow.com/

Here's a place to get a Twitter Badge - https://twitter.com/logo and there are many others like this one - http://www.twittericon.com/. Just choose a design, type your Twitter name in the box, and it will generate the code. Then copy and paste the html text code below the image you like, and when you insert it as a widget/gadget on your website or blog, it will become a cute birdie picture that people click to follow you.

http://www.twitter.com/

LinkedIn.

LinkedIn is the largest professional social networking site in the world. It's not just a place to put your resume, but there are other things going on at LinkedIn. With 135 million people from over 200 countries and territories, it's too large not to be a part of. At LinkedIn you can manage your public profile that's available for everyone to see, find and get introduced to people with connections in your specialty field and join groups very similar to Facebook. You can also be found for business opportunities, partners needed and join in discussions with likeminded individuals in private group settings. It's a smart social media site. Another bonus to being a LinkedIn member, as with Facebook, is that you'll be able to reconnect with old friends that you haven't spoken with in ages. That's a nice benefit as you're working on your online presence!

http://www.linkedin.com/

Other People's Blogs (OPB).

Other people write and update blogs constantly. These blogs are on every subject under the sun and usually have comment boxes where visitors can leave replies and continue the discussion. *This is perhaps the best method for regularly getting your URL links out there.* However, you must use White Hat methods and leave thoughtful comments that add to the discussion.

Not only do blogs get read by many visitors for years to come, but the comments get read as well. Comment boxes often ask for a URL to go along with your message. When your sites are ready, you'll always want to insert the URL address so that people who read the comment can click on your link.

It's mandatory to have something that adds to the discussion. Showing you can assist or entertain others will do much more to get people to click on your link. You can also type out the full URL address within the comment box that typically will become a clickable link.

Note that comments often require approval from the blog owner before they get published. But as long as it's something useful *blog owners usually approve comments because they want it to appear that many people read their blog.* Once your comment is posted it will act like a billboard for your site for years to come. One smart blog comment and link can literally attract hundreds or even thousands of visitors to your site over time. It's not an exaggeration to say that many thousands of clicks per year are attainable by simply making three smart blog comments per day.

So how do you find all these blogs where you'd like to leave comments?

Google Alerts.

We talked about them before. This is not a social media site but a social media tool. Google Alerts are incredibly helpful for anyone marketing online. I use them for my book titles, for my name and also for subjects of interest like self-publishing and ebooks.

To get started, visit the site - http://www.google.com/alerts and fill out the form with your search terms and information. Google will email you with any web content that appears. Then visit those articles and blog posts. If there's a comment box, leave a thoughtful reply and insert your URL which will be a clickable part of your name next to the comment. You can often type in a URL in the comment area itself that will become clickable. I recommend leaving at least three comments per day so the potential for new visitors will increase dramatically over the following weeks and months.

Comments often require the moderator to approve them, but blog hosts usually do because it shows that people read their blog. No bloggers enjoy seeing their comment boxes reading zero, even me.

Forums in General.

Whatever the subject of your website is about, it's a pretty sure bet there are forums dedicated to that somewhere. Find these forums and participate. For example, a simple Google search for "model airplane forums" or "model airplanes" should result in places to meet and great likeminded people.

You can also create forums within your website which is a brilliant way to network with others.

There are hundreds of other social media sites and tools. Because this field is growing exponentially, I'm only going to discuss and touch on a few of them.

YouTube.com.

You might not think of this at first as a place to promote your website but it's a great way to drive traffic, especially if you're fairly handy with video. A simple video about you and your site can be seen by hundreds to thousands of people in little time. Watch some YouTube videos on similar subjects to get a feel for what others are doing and decide if those ideas might work for you. Some people talk about services and products for sale. Others discuss what they're about and how to find them. For my YouTube videos, I give examples of free advice on making websites and ebooks and include the URLs for those interested in learning more. The nice thing about these videos is the amount of views they get and the fact that some people relate better to video than to text ads. Re-read the previous advice I gave on steps to take for YouTube in the Video and Video SEO chapter.

Even if you're not making a video, YouTube is also a place to leave comments similar to blog comments although they tend to get bumped down the list quickly over time (depending on how popular the video is). You can't leave URL links as easily as for blogs, but you can mention your site and cleverly leave a URL as just the domain name. Again, make sure to leave helpful or entertaining comments and not come across like a spammer.

Definitely consider possibilities with YouTube in terms of blurbs about your sites in ways that might gather some traffic. There are also badges for YouTube or you can create links to your profile page. You can also embed YouTube videos into your blog and website by copying and pasting the HTML code beneath the video. This is also smart for SEO rankings because the videos contain a large amount of data, and one factor Google considers important is the data size of your website.

http://www.youtube.com

Pinterest.com

Pinterest is all about sharing photos and images, typically within a theme, that others can also "repin," which is akin to retweeting for Twitter. Their mission is to connect people world-wide with similar interests and ideas. Pinterest should be considered by anyone with lots of imagery.

http://www.pinterest.com

Yahoo Answers.

Yahoo has an enormous forum under the title of Yahoo Answers. Both questions and answers exist from people all over the world for every subject imaginable. There are sections like environment, pets, health, sports, travel, business, arts, books, family, games, food/drink and many more.

You can browse the most recent questions or search for questions pertaining to your subjects. Then it's good to answer the question in a helpful manner. You can also leave a

URL link within the answer box or the resource box. The good thing about Yahoo Answers is that they act as blog posts where people researching questions for months and years later can still stumble upon your answer, especially if it's chosen as the best answer and placed in the top of the results. Be sure to look for recent questions that are unresolved by tailoring the search to be for Open Question posts in the Question Status.

http://answers.yahoo.com/

Others to consider:

http://www.flickr.com/ - for sharing images.

http://www.digg.com/ - general social site and place where you can recommend blogs and sites.

http://www.metacafe.com/ - videos.

http://www.stumbleupon.com/ - discover cool stuff.

http://www.technorati.com/ - a collection of blogs and a great place to search for blogs of interest. You can also write articles for Technorati, something I've found to be very beneficial.

http://www.delicious.com/ - general social site.

There are literally hundreds of others. One could write several books on this topic alone, so please understand if I haven't mentioned a social media site you enjoy. But even partially doing what I've recommended, these venues will be of tremendous value as you create links to your blog and websites. You don't have to be super-active or try to do them all, nor would I recommend it, but make sure your URL links are in at least three of these and use Google Alerts.

GOGFP Step #18. Use Social Media sites to promote your URL and websites. Make sure to complete a Google Plus profile with a face shot.

PR (Public Relations)

What do you do once everything's in place? That's the time to lean back and watch the traffic roll in as the rankings start climbing to page one, right? Wrong. As visitors come to your sites, Google will take notice but the SEO efforts are ongoing. Do what you can over time with consistent bits of effort to draw more traffic. Marketing online is about patience, persistence and determination. **These things take time**. Be prepared to put in continued devotion even after everything is in place.

The good news is that you're in the homestretch and just need some occasional persistence to keep the word out about your websites. Eventually, assuming people like what you're doing, a buzz will generate from others who will actually help with the marketing by writing about your site and referring it to others.

Press releases.

Press releases are great ways to get the word out about your sites and products. There are many companies that offer free press release services, and you can even submit a similar but slightly altered press release to a few different ones. I do not recommend copying and pasting the exact same press release to multiple venues, as that may come back to you unfavorably (but you can try it, just don't tell them I said to).

The companies will each have more specifics on how to write and submit a professional press release. Some general things to consider are that these are not supposed to sound like promotions; they're meant to sound like news copy, what's happening and why it's interesting. Submitting a release that reads, "I have an awesome website and everyone should visit because…" is not going to fly. Similar in rule to companies like Ezinearticles.com (see below), press releases should answer the questions like what, when, how and why this matters, and not be a big sales pitch.

Here are some companies that offer free versions of press releases:

PR.com
Free-press-release.com
1888pressrelease.com
PRlog.org

Write and Submit Articles.

If you can write the content within your webpages, you can write short articles. These can be articles about your sites and products/services, or they can be subjects that interest you. Like press releases, submitting articles is a great way to get your URL links out there. Remember to be professional when writing articles and have them polished and of quality content. Then submit articles to anywhere you can for free. You can even submit the exact same article to multiple places, maybe with minor alterations to each in the title and the first sentence or paragraph to help distinguish them. Here are some great places, and again more can be found with a Google search:

http://www.goarticles.com/ - the self-proclaimed largest free content article directory. I really like them in that the articles post fairly quickly, usually within 48 hours, and they aren't too fussy with rules. They send a confirmation email once posted, as does Ezines and IdeaMarketers. To see examples of articles I've written for this service visit here - http://www.goarticles.com/cgi-bin/author.cgi?C=282217.

http://www.ezinearticles.com/ - expert authors sharing their articles. This site takes a bit longer and is much stricter on following all of their rules for accepting articles but is really a great place once you get the hang of it. Your article must sound unbiased and not promotional whatsoever (the real problem with many of my own submissions). If your articles are denied, which happened to me plenty of times, don't worry. They'll explain exactly why and let you make alterations until you get approved.

These are just a few but plenty to get started with. One thing you'll discover is that your articles will get picked up by other online magazines and ran without your knowledge. This is terrific in that your URLs are getting distributed and inserted by other people, like someone else working SEO for you for free.

GOGFP Step #19. Use PR (public relations) by submitting articles and press releases on a regular basis after everything is in place.

Fix the Problems

This should go without saying, but it's important to make sure everything works on your website. Check that the navigation goes where it should, the outbound links work properly, the pages load relatively quickly, etc. Test your links occasionally to make sure things work and if they don't, fix them.

Custom 404 Error Page.

A 404 Error Page is what a user sees when trying to access a non-existent URL address. It may be that the user misspelled the address, clicked on a misspelled link or the webpage no longer exists though its links are still out there. By default, 404 pages just tell the user that the page doesn't exist and offer little else to go on. Though the recommended solutions differ a bit, the common opinion is that 404s are not great for user experience and thus not good for SEO either.

For example, let's say a website has a certain page called musclecars.com/67-corvette and someone accidentally types in musclecars.com/67-corvete or perhaps another webmaster even creates a hyperlink to the misspelling. When the user tries to load that page they will go through the musclecars.com webserver to find a page that doesn't exist. Or maybe after a bad accident, the actual website's owner decided he/she no longer likes the '67 Corvette and removed that page entirely even though hundreds of links to it still exist in Cyberspace. Because Google wants to provide a pleasant user experience, they have taught the spiders to report 404 error pages and deem them bad news.

Clearly, you don't want 404s, especially if it can be helped. It's in your power to always make sure the URL hyperlinks work when leaving them on your own site or elsewhere. It's also in your control to create 301 redirects when you decide to delete a page or website. It's not in your power to make sure everyone correctly spells a URL. What you don't want those users to find is a standard 404 error page that gives the visitor no information, *and they simply leave your site.*

There are three main choices for a webmaster:

- Just say *what the heck* and do nothing (not recommended). It's surprising how common this is.

- Create a 301 redirect that responds to all 404 error pages and automatically sends the user to another page on the site like the homepage (quasi-recommended). At least the user is still at your site but she/he might feel confused.

- Create a custom 404 page that explains to the user that an error has occurred while offering some potential solutions. This should look like a normal page with navigation or a sitemap (most recommended). The custom page can also request users to report the broken link to help make the webmaster (you) aware of it. Additionally, it can contain a Google Search box (html widget) to allow the user to search by terms they were looking for.

This decision is affected by what your needs are, but I'd rarely recommend a 301 redirect (which I'll explain below) and primarily recommend a custom 404 error page. The most common custom 404 is simply a page that looks like a normal page, and it explains the error as being an invalid choice along with better link options present. It's a user-friendly way of letting people know how to access your website, instead of hoping they'll find a way to return. To see a custom 404 example at one of my sites, visit http://www.thelittleuniverse.com/, and then once the page has loaded type in a random set of letters or numbers after the .com/ part (make sure there is a forward slash "/" following .com as in .com/sh5x9iu) and hit enter. It should go to my 404 page.

To add this custom 404 page, you'll need access to the inner workings of your site which will not happen with most free websites. (Fortunately, it's automatically provided by blogs like wordpress.com and blogger.com, which is a nice feature.) You'll also need to feel comfortable working on the website behind the scenes or have your webmaster do this, like making alterations with the File Manager in cPanel for example. Whenever doing these things for the first times, *it's a good idea to copy and save the existing information before making changes,* so that previous info can be replaced if needed.

For websites that run on Apache servers, you'll need to find your .htaccess file (look in the hidden files when opening the public_html web root directory). If you don't have this file already, you can use Notepad to create and add a New

Folder and name it .htaccess (just like that with the period in front). Within the .htaccess folder, you can type the following code exactly as it appears, matching case and spaces around the 404: ErrorDocument 404 /notfound.html. In the next paragraph we'll discussing adding a 301 redirect here as well, and the two codes can be used simultaneously. Save that in the .htaccess folder.

Now, you'll also need to create or add a New File and name it notfound.html for the custom 404 to work. After creating that file you can edit it to say whatever you want on a 404 error page. It's a good idea to make the page similar to others or to your home page. I usually copy and paste the HTML code of my home page (index.html) which contains the navigation items and then edit out the page text and replace it with something like this: *Whoops, this page doesn't exist. Please return to the home page or to another in the navigation bar.* You can also visit several websites and purposely misspell the suffix of their URL to see how they handle (or not) 404 errors.

For websites that run on other servers than Apache you'll need to check with the individual program by Googling something like "create custom 404 error page for *fill in the blank* servers."

301 Redirect, part 1 for www versus non-www.

Ever notice how it doesn't matter if you include the www or not in a URL address? The website still loads. However, it does matter for SEO if it goes to both the www and non-www versions. Confused? I was.

This is known as a Canonical URL issue. If you type into the browser either www.yourdomain.com or just yourdomain.com, do they both go to the respective URL you typed or do they revert to either one after loading? I'm not talking about the same website; does the URL address in the browser still read exactly as you typed it in after loading the webpage?

For example, if your site is called www.teengossip.com and it can be typed either way, with or without the www and that wording goes to exactly the respective URL, then it's splitting your SEO efforts in half. Perhaps my daughter has a hyperlink to http://www.teengossip.com on her blog while her best friend has a hyperlink to http://teengossip.com; Google will only see that as one link to each URL instead of two links to the same website. The latter is better for SEO.

How this came to pass I'm not really sure, but Google advises a 301 permanent redirect to make the non-www website point to the other. That way, the spiders will only find one website in the future and give it all the SEO credit instead of splitting the credit in half.

One quick way to check is to type in each version, one with the www and one without, and see if they both show up as the same URL for your website or blog. For example, I have two blogs that automatically redirect without me having to do anything. If someone types in http://thebigbangauthor.com it automatically shows up as http://www.thebigbangauthor.com. Similarly, if someone types in http://www.ebooksuccess4free.wordpress.com it automatically goes to http://ebooksuccess4free.wordpress.com.

This was not the case with my paid-for hosted websites, where both the www version and the non-www lead to their respective locales. What did I do about it? There was a fairly simple fix to apply a 301 permanent redirect. It involves accessing the hidden files within your public_html settings and then adding a simple code to the .htaccess file. This should only be attempted by someone familiar with working on their own website, and even then *it's a good idea to copy and save the existing information before making changes,* so that previous info can be replaced if needed.

For websites that run Apache servers, which is the majority, the code to add to the .htaccess file looks like this:

RewriteEngine On

RewriteCond %{HTTP_HOST} ^example.com

RewriteRule (.*) http://www.example.com/$1 [R=301,L]

And you would need to substitute your domain name for both instances of the word *example*.

For websites that run Microsoft servers, the code to add to the .htaccess file looks like this:

< %@ Language=VBScript %>

< %

Response.Status="301 Moved Permanently"

Response.AddHeader   "Location",
http://www.example.com

%>

Here is a great site for a further tutorial -

http://www.stepforth.com/resources/web-marketing-knowledgebase/non-www-redirect/

GOGFP Step #20. Make sure your website functions properly and add a custom 404 error page for improper URL entries along with a 301 permanent redirect for www versus non-www issues.

301 Redirect (optional), part 2 for URL domain name changes.

In addition to utilizing a 301 permanent redirect (see above) to solve canonical www versus non-www issues, it can be used when changing a domain name entirely. This is optional, but if your URL domain name is not keyword optimized and **the site isn't performing well,** it should be seriously considered. *A new URL that is optimized for keywords will greatly outperform one that isn't* in as short as a few weeks. Over time the difference will likely translate to more visitors in the tens of thousands to potentially millions.

From Google; *if you need to change the URL of a page as it is shown in search engine results, we recommended that you use a server-side 301 redirect. This is the best way to ensure that users and search engines are directed to the correct page. The 301 status code means that a page has permanently moved to a new location.*

301 redirects are particularly useful in the following circumstances:

You've moved your site to a new domain, *and you want to make the transition as seamless as possible.*

People access your site through several different URLs. If, for example, your home page can be reached in multiple ways - for instance, http://example.com/home, http://home.example.com, or http://www.example.com - it's a good idea to pick one of those URLs as your preferred (canonical) destination, and use 301 redirects to send traffic from the other URLs to your preferred URL. You can also use Webmaster Tools to set your preferred domain.

You're merging two websites and want to make sure that links to outdated URLs are redirected to the correct pages.

To implement a 301 redirect for websites that are hosted on servers running Apache, you'll need access to your server's .htaccess file. (If you're not sure about your access or your server software, check with your webhoster.) For more information, consult the Apache .htaccess Tutorial and the Apache URL Rewriting Guide. If your site is hosted on a server running other software, check with your hoster for more details.

Even though this is actually a simple thing to do (I discovered by doing one), implementing a 301 redirect can feel like a daunting task for many people. Because of that reason, **this should either be done by a webdesigner or by someone comfortably working on their site.** The goal is to make it as user-friendly for people visiting your old site's URL *and* for maintaining/transferring the SEO results from that old site to the new one. The instructions below are for Apache servers and .htaccess redirects which are by far the most common scenarios. If you have another operating system, it will be necessary to find the proper tutorial. Here's a list of helpful resources for those wanting further study:

http://googlewebmastercentral.blogspot.com/2008/04/best-practices-when-moving-your-site.html

http://en.wikipedia.org/wiki/URL_redirection

http://www.webconfs.com/how-to-redirect-a-webpage.php - for many methods and scenarios of 301 redirects.

For example, let's say you want to do a 301 redirect for a completely new domain name like switching from (old) cutelittlebirdiebath.com to (new) solarbirdbath.com. Obviously you must first register the new domain name and have it hosted. You will also need to create the website and its pages, even if it is with the same duplicated pages that you'll be redirecting from the old domain. Again the directions below are for Apache servers (which is what the majority of people have) and you can check this tutorial of others for additional servers - http://www.webconfs.com/how-to-redirect-a-webpage.php.

To move all of the contents of one domain name to another, either edit your existing .htaccess file or create a blank ".htaccess" file (open Notepad and save the file as .htaccess). The .htaccess file goes in the same root directory as your index file which is the home page. Copy and paste the following code to the first lines of that file (adding in the URL of your new domain name):

Options +FollowSymLinks

RewriteEngine on

RewriteRule (.*) http://www.newdomain.com/$1 [R=301,L]

So for our example, we'd edit the top lines of the .htaccess file within the old site, cutelittlebirdiebath.com, to read like this:

Options +FollowSymLinks

RewriteEngine on

RewriteRule (.*) http://www.solarbirdbath.com/$1 [R=301,L]

Now when anyone types in cutelittlebirdiebath.com or clicks on a hyperlink for it, they will be redirected to solarbirdbath.com. *This also works for the individual pages and files so long as they are named the same thing at solarbirdbath.com.*

(If everything is in place and the 301 redirect isn't working, make sure MOD Rewrite is on. It should be by default. Look for a file called httpd.conf that resides on your server. Within it, the following line should exist: LoadModule rewrite_module modules/mod_rewrite.so)

Unfortunately, when you 301 redirect an old domain to a new one, you'll initially have to keep paying for the annual domain renewal and hosting of the old domain name. Eventually, once the 301 registers and the majority of backlinks to the old URL are corrected or gone, you can delete the old domain and hosting account. You should probably not remove the old account if the URL still gets substantial direct type-in traffic.

Crawl Errors.

These errors occur when Google is told something exists and tries to crawl a page or file but can't access it. They are largely 404 errors. Using Webmaster Tools will help identify where Google is finding crawl errors, and those files and/or pages should be either deleted or fixed.

What if you believe you've been banned from Google's index?

This should only happen for a site that has an HTML code that is keeping it from being indexed, is a duplicate content site, is caught practicing Black Hat tactics or has such tasteless or useless content that Google decides not to index it. Hopefully it won't ever happen.

Usually when a site isn't coming up in a search result, it's simply because it hasn't yet been indexed. For new sites or URLs, this can take up to a few weeks. You can always check by typing the exact URL into a search box, as in http://example.com, and seeing if it's listed in the first results. If not, it's probably just waiting to be indexed and you can try resubmitting it to Google directly at https://www.google.com/webmasters/tools/home?hl=en. You can also check to see a site's status by several banned checker tools like this one - http://www.bannedcheck.com/.

If your site truly has been banned, you should first check to make sure it's not a robot.txt file or another reason where all of the webpages have been placed under the "do not crawl" protocol. I discuss the robot.txt function in the next chapter for those who need more info. If the robot.txt file or meta tags have been changed, they could direct the spiders to exclude your site. Simply check your robot.txt file (if you have one) and your meta tags. You should never read this in your meta tags: <meta name="ROBOTS" content="NOINDEX">. If that's the case, your site is blocked from Google.

Or you could have a robots.txt with incorrect code. The example that follows allows all robots to visit all files because the wildcard "*" specifies all robots.

User-agent: *

Disallow:

This next example keeps all robots out:

User-agent: *

Disallow: /

For much more explanations on this, visit here - http://en.wikipedia.org/wiki/Robots.txt and here - http://www.robotstxt.org/.

You can also check to see if someone has copied your website and placed a duplicate site online. In this case, Google will just index one of them. Check by searching for an exact line of text in the page body.

Next is to determine if it's a Black Hat issue by going over your strategies and checking for issues like overuse of keyword stuffing. Make alterations (if needed) and resubmit.

The final resort is to contact Google's support department - https://support.google.com/ and see if they can identify the problem and present solutions.

Other Things You Can Do

Some of what follows is about analyzing your SEO efforts, and some is about driving traffic. Either way, both are good things to do to keep moving forward. Here's a note of forewarning about the companies that grade your website and blog; *take the results with a grain of salt* as you work to make corrections. For example, one of my websites that scores the highest with these programs also receives comparatively lower traffic and is currently working to make the front page of Google. Conversely, one of my sites that receives the lowest grade happens to have the best traffic and has landed of page one of Google for well over 1,000 search terms. That's right; my lowest graded site actually does the best in traffic, SEO and converting the most customers. Weird.

http://www.webceo.com/ - This company claims to be the most complete SEO software package on the planet, and they may be right. It also has a free program to download containing in-depth website analysis and educational videos/literature. In fact, it has so much content and evaluations that *it may be way more than most people want to delve into*. It's amazing that this much assistance is free, and it certainly entices many customers to upgrade to their paid programs (although I think if anyone uses the free versions

111

wisely along or the other advice I give here, they'll be just fine).

http://upcity.com/free-tools/seo-report-card - This is a similar service, and it has the extra feature of inserting your main keywords and a competitor's URL to see how you're stacking up.

Find out who links to you.

By typing this into a Google search box, link://yourdomain.com/, a list of websites will appear that all have links to yours. This is a great way to check up on some of your SEO efforts as well as make pleasant discoveries and connections. I like to randomly visit these websites and make comments if there are boxes. Plus it's fun to see your efforts coming to fruition.

Experiment with Google searches for your own keywords.

What happens when you search for your name or the main keywords your website is promoting? Do you come up on page one, five, fifteen or not at all. Make a list and monitor your results. Use your statistics monitoring or Google Analytics to check in on the keyword searches that visitors have used to find your website. You can also perform searches with Bing to compare results, which might be surprisingly different. (Also remember to clear your internet history so the search results aren't affected by cookies and things like that.)

Update your site on a regular basis.

Keeping your sites fresh with recent material will assist with new visitors and past members returning as well as getting the search engines to notice you. Search engines will check on your site as they regularly do, and they rank sites higher if they have recently updated information. For your blog this shouldn't be a problem, as you should add a new entry or update at least once a week in addition to posting comments from visitors. For your website, even a mere change of a new paragraph, video or link qualifies as an update. Do this every few months to keep the search engines noticing new info.

Robot.txt Function.

Even though this book focuses on getting Google to notice your pages, *there may be some pages on your site that you don't want them to crawl or index.* For example, maybe you have a download page for an ebook that you don't want made public.

For disallowing the robots on certain pages on your site, you can use the robots.txt code that will tell the spiders not to crawl certain pages. There is a thorough tutorial here - http://www.robotstxt.org/robotstxt.html or online with a search. In general, it works like a custom 404 error page or a 301 permanent redirect. For cPanel users, you need access to the file manager, Web Root directory public_html/www where you can find the robots.txt file. Viewing it will look something like this:

User-agent: *
Disallow: /_mm/
Disallow: /_notes/
Disallow: /_baks/

Disallow: /MMWIP/

User-agent: googlebot
Disallow: *.csi

If you have certain pages that you don't want crawled and indexed, they need to be added here. For example, if you don't want the webpage for the '67 Corvette made public you could have the line, Disallow:/67-corvette/ included in the top section. These restrictions can be set for either exclusions or allowances, for the entire website, for individual search engines and for individual pages or even files.

Review List of **GOGFP** Steps

Since there are many Get On Google Front Page Steps, here's the review list for reference:

Step #1. Provide great content. Make your website the very best it can be so others will visit, spend time, share and link to it.

Step #2. Be patient and treat SEO like a diet or exercise program. It takes time, and the results will be great if you remain persistent.

Step #3. Use the Keyword Planner to optimize at least 6 to 10 keyword terms. These should be both short and long-tail to be used later accordingly.

Step #4. This is arguably the most important lesson. Optimize your URL domain name to include your best short-tail keywords. It's okay if these keywords are competitive since you are in this for the duration.

Step #5. Blog regularly, weekly or bi-weekly if you can. Even brief posts under 400 words will lead visitors to any site. Use short-tail keywords for categories, tags and labels, while using long-tail keywords for the titles of posts and the accompanying text.

Step #6. Get comfortable viewing page source and looking for elements within that are related to SEO.

Step #7. Optimize your HTML title <title> information for up to 66 characters with a few keywords from high to low priority that reads like a headline.

Step #8. Optimize your Meta Description to be up to 150 characters, with several keywords generally from high to low priority, and good for human readers to attract clicks.

Step #9. Make sure your sites have the HTML code edited to include your title, meta description and (optional) keywords. Also add an H1 title tag if it's not there already. Then check the Page Source to make sure they are all in.

Step #10. Use short and long-tail keywords in the text of the page body while paying attention to Density, Frequency, Prominence and Proximity. You can also use bold text to emphasize Prominence.

Step #11. Freely submit your URL directly to Google. You should also do Bing, DMOZ and ScrubTheWeb while considering other places optional.

Step #12. Verify your sites directly with Google. Others are optional.

Step #13. Submit a sitemap to Google, and optimize the ease with which visitors navigate your webpages.

Step #14. Use every free Google program that is related to your projects, especially Analytics, Alerts and Webmaster Tools.

Step #15. Always leave your URL in a hyperlinked method whenever and wherever you can to continually plant backlinks like Johnny Appleseed.

Step #16. Always use alternative text (alt text) to accompany your images. Consider title attributes optional.

Step #17. Submit video sitemaps directly to Google to enable direct links to your URL from video search results.

Step #18. Use Social Media sites to promote your URL and websites. Make sure to complete a Google Plus profile with a face shot.

Step #19. Use PR (public relations) by submitting articles and press releases on a regular basis after everything is in place.

Step #20. Make sure your website functions properly and add a custom 404 error page for improper URL entries along with a 301 permanent redirect for www versus non-www issues.

Cheating With Money

At the time this book was first published in January of 2011, I had never spent money on SEO. Part of the reason is I'm too cheap to try it while another part is that I like experimenting for free and watching the results. Since then I tried a bit of AdWords with Google and didn't have very good results so I discontinued that. Fortunately success is coming pretty well with the free stuff, so why spend more money? I also like being an example as if to say, "I'm doing it with free methods and you can too."

However, that doesn't mean trying a pay-per-click (PPC) campaign, for example, isn't a wise thing to do. There may come a time where you'd like to spend money *wisely* to make some of these SEO efforts better or add things that aren't available for free. I totally understand. With that in mind, as the epilogue to this book, I'd like to include a few things that I believe will make sense eventually to some.

AdWords and Pay Per Click advertising on Google.

Google has a range of possibilities with advertising on any budget. You can spend small amounts or large ones and see if the results are worth it. The nice thing is that you only pay when your advertising works, when someone clicks the ad and either visits your site or buys a product. I still advise immersing yourself in all the free methods from this book first, but Google does have a nice program here - https://adwords.google.com/.

Hiring a professional SEO outfit.

Although I truly believe the bulk of the most important items are covered here, this could still be an option for those with deeper pockets, limited time and greater expectations. It is true that I am just one opinion, and there are professional outfits that know a lot more than I do. They could help with the myriad of little things which might be what you really need to get over the hump. *My advice is to practice everything I have taught here first.* If you still need help, then either assess what you've been doing, contact me for free advice or pay for SEO services which are likely not going to be cheap.

The End

(Side note—if any customer of this book would also like a free pdf version that might be handier on her/his computer with all the hyperlinks, just let me know. I don't have any way of verifying who bought the book through a retailer other than if she/he left a review, so if that sounds fair just direct me to the review and receive a free pdf copy. Email jason@thelittleuniverse.com with *free pdf for my review* in the subject box. Even if you don't want the pdf, ***it would be greatly appreciated if you would be so kind as to leave an honest review.***)

That's it for now. I sincerely hope you'll put these elements into practice and find your time and effort rewarded with good SER, successful sites and a satisfying online career.

Please keep in mind, online marketing typically is not a get-rich-quick scheme. It will take time. Search engines can take months to really notice you. Being successful with SEO will require patience, persistence and perseverance to drive traffic in numbers that make you happy. I hope you'll remember this whenever you're feeling frustrated by the process, as I have felt many, many times.

Thank you again for reading. I wish you the best of success. Please contact me through the websites if you have further comments and questions.

Kind regards and best wishes,
-Jason

About the Author

Jason Matthews was born in North Carolina in 1967. He graduated from UNC-Chapel Hill with a degree in film and television. Jason lives in Pismo Beach, California, where he writes and teaches self-publishing.

He asks readers to **please leave reviews** at Amazon or anywhere you found the book.

He can be contacted through his websites, TheLittleUniverse.com - ebooksuccess4free.webs.com.

Facebook - facebook.com/Jason.M.Matthews

Google Plus - plus.google.com/+JasonMatthews

Twitter - twitter.com/Jason_Matthews

Where applicable, it helps to send a personal note. Thank you.

Other Books by Jason Matthews

The following are available as ebooks and paperbacks at major retailers.

Better You, Better Me - there's a better version of you ready to be energized. The ideas in this book are easy to add to your life, and they work wonders.

The Little Universe - a novel about creating a universe and discovering incredible things within it.

Jim's Life - the sequel novel, about a teenage boy on trial who can see and heal the human light fields, being hailed a miracle healer as the world argues over his case.

How to Make, Market and Sell Ebooks All for Free – self publish on any budget and sell ebooks at major retailers, your own sites on autopilot and much more.

How to Make Your Own Free Website: And Your Free Blog Too - a how to book for building free websites/blogs and making the most with them.

Get On Google Front Page - dedicated to SEO tips, using Google better and rising in search engine rankings.

Please enjoy a sample chapter of *How to Make Your Own Free Website: And Your Free Blog Too.*

The List of Free Website Companies

I'm going to make a list of website companies that offer both of these important things: free hosting and site-building tools. In the following chapter, I'll do the same thing for blogging companies. After listing them, I'll go into greater details with the ones I recommend you use. However, you may decide another company is right for your needs and that's okay. The tutorial will still *basically* be the same for any company as this is quickly turning into *universal* terms. In order for you to decide what's in your best interest, it makes sense to see what's out there before jumping into the very first one.

This is a partial list first written in September of 2010, updated regularly and most recently in September of 2014 because things change quickly in the industry. There are new companies coming out all the time and dozens that I haven't mentioned here. Please be aware of those facts, although I do believe the venues that follow are the best for most people. These sites typically require users to be at least 13 years of age, that the sites do not contain profanity or pornography and that other common decencies are followed.

(Also it should be noted all of these sites have introductory options that are totally free, while if you want to upgrade for things like more storage space, personalized domain name, more pages, no ads in some cases, email accounts, etc.—that can also be done for very reasonable prices.)

Here's the list of free website companies I recommend you try out:

Webs.com.

This was formerly called Freewebs.com and not to be confused with Web.com, which did not make my recommended list.

Webs.com is among the all-around best companies for creating free websites. I've personally created three websites through them including one of the examples for this book, http://your-own-free-website.webs.com. They have so many pros going for them such as a great site-building program, hundreds of templates to choose from, every type of widget and add-on you should ever need, a knowledge forum of support consisting of other members, customized apps and more. I've never had a major problem with them, and the few times I've had minor problems they've always been cleared up within 24 hours. From their site;

At Webs, we provide all the tools you need to create a professional-looking website in just minutes. Add a blog, forum, calendar, photo gallery, video gallery and much more. Want to turn your site into a social network? No problem! You also have the ability to add members and create personal profiles so you can turn your site into a community where friends, colleagues and family can connect and collaborate.

The free version at Webs.com currently gives you about 42MB of storage space and a bandwidth capacity of 500MB. To put some perspective on that, everything a visitor clicks on or downloads takes from the monthly bandwidth. Pictures, files, etc., things that get clicked on all slowly deplete your monthly allotment of bandwidth resource. For starting out, this bandwidth allotment should be fine for most anyone. If you have massive amounts if video or visitors, you may want to look into an upgrade at a reasonable price or another venue, like Yola below.

Perhaps the main complaint with Webs.com free sites is the one small forced ad on the side of your webpage. This is not a pop-up but just a small ad. For me, this is not a big deal as I see ads on Facebook, YouTube, Yahoo, ESPN and just about every other world-class site I frequently visit. The ad is always chosen to be in line with the subjects of your site, making them even more tolerable. However if signing up for AdSense by Google is something you'll insist on doing, then the free Webs.com program will not work. You may have to use another service or upgrade to a Premium package for $4/month if you absolutely have to remove the forced ad and make way for something like AdSense (which is a requirement by AdSense for any webhosting company: no additional ads on the page).

I use Webs (and Yola) for examples and therefore go into great detail for them specifically. If you research online you'll find people who love Webs.com and people who don't, but I promise you there are way more people who love them. Of course if you choose another company, that's fine too. My advice will work with any of these below.

Yola.com.

Yola is one of the best places to make free websites and they have no ads. If you do the research, you'll hear a lot of satisfied customers who built sites at Yola.com, formerly called Synthasite and based in San Francisco. I have built an example site at http://yourownfreewebsite.yolasite.com. If you visit the site you'll notice this is the one that I spent a few bucks for the custom domain name, http://your-own-free-website.com. This is what the company says about Yola;

With Yola, if you can edit a document, you can build a free website. Yola's award-winning support team is always available, making websites easy to manage and simple to change. Yola packages include over 100 ad-free customizable templates, so you can create a website you'll love without annoying pop-ups. Yola gives you the features you want, including integration with YouTube, Google Maps, and PayPal. With Yola, you'll get two free websites with 1GB of storage so you can claim your rightful place on the web. You can purchase your own custom domain name, or decide to use a subdomain that comes with the free website hosting Yola provides. Yola's award-winning support team is always available to not only walk you through the steps to make a free website, but also to provide tips and tricks for making your website stand out and give you a website you're proud of.

What a like about Yola is the lack of a forced ad (that's right, no ad for the free version) and the extra storage space.

1GB (gigabyte) of storage is a lot, especially for those who have ample amounts of video and/or audio to present. Drag and drop features make it incredibly easy for anyone to build the pages. They also have a Properties tab on each page for Keywords and SEO tools, a great support staff and forum of helpful people. Additionally, Yola is a great choice for those who want a free site including AdSense by Google for extra income potential.

Weebly.com.

Like Yola, Weebly.com also has drag and drop editing. It comes with over 70 templates, the same content components as the others, and there are no forced ads so AdSense is a possibility. It also has an easy to use SEO tab for adding custom keywords, headers and footers. Many users love Weebly, and its reviews are generally very good. From their site;

Building a website on Weebly is unlike anything you've ever experienced. Our drag & drop website builder makes it dead simple to create a powerful, professional website without any technical skills required. Over 6 million people and small businesses have joined Weebly to build their online presence.

Content elements (like text, photos, maps, and videos) are added to your website by simply dragging & dropping them into place. Text is edited just like in a word processor. Building your website is done in real time, right from within your web browser. There's absolutely nothing to install and no upgrades to worry about.

As usual with all venues, I found some complaints as well but most happy users. Check them out and see what you think.

Webstarts.com

Drag and drop features, e-commerce and SEO optimization are among the main points the venue discusses for their free sites. 5GB of monthly bandwidth is huge but 10MB of storage isn't much compared to most others. Webstarts also limits the free sites to 5 separate webpages, which could be ample for some people. This might include pages like Home, About Us, E-Store, Contact and Links for example.

Google Sites.

What I like about this outfit is that it's run by Google, the king of most things internet. What I don't like about the venue is the lack of introductory material (as of this writing) for beginners to get a sense of what it's all about. First-time visitors are merely greeted with a page that asks you to input a URL and choose a template without any tutorial video or text meant to assist the process. It's like a wham-bam-thank-you-ma'am introduction. They do offer a good size of monthly bandwidth at 100MB and are obviously designed to be used with anything on Google like AdSense. Because Google is so important for everything online, Google Sites should be considered as a valuable option for free venues. If you want more info, watch a few tutorial videos at YouTube on making Google Sites or Google Sites tutorial.

Forumotion.com

This venue is specifically designed for people who want to create forums. Even though the other venues I mentioned have pages that can be customized for forums or member's areas, what Forumotion is doing is somewhat unique. They offer unlimited forum users and messages, domain name and customized email addresses, over 3000 templates and a huge support forum to help with questions. If strictly building a forum is the main purpose for your site, then Forumotion is a great way to go.

Etsy.com.

Etsy is a community and a company of buyers and sellers. They are made up primarily of artists selling everything from sculpture to wedding accessories. From Etsy's home page;

Our mission is to enable people to make a living making things, and to reconnect makers with buyers. Our vision is to build a new economy and present a better choice.

Etsy makes it easy for anyone to set up shop and begin selling products. There's no registration fee to get started. They charge modest fees for listing an item (20 cents per item) and take a small cut of any sale (3.5% transaction fee).

Etsy is a great way to go for artists who simply want to add their products to existing sales templates. Additionally, artists who use Etsy will benefit from the tremendous amount of daily visitors that are already aware of the site. One idea for this type of person is to create an Etsy store as well as their own website or blog. Why not, especially when it's free?

Deviantart.com

This is similar to Etsy, but DeviantART is tailored to art that is more digital and less physical. DeviantART attracts painters, photographers, game makers, designers, film makers, animators, poets, writers and more. They claim over

100 million original works of art from over 19 million users and 45 million people per month visiting. You can set up a profile, create a gallery, connect with art-lovers around the world and sell your work.

Wetpaint.com

Wetpaint specializes in wiki websites. These are sites that can be edited and contributed to by everyone who visits the site like Wikipedia, the free online encyclopedia edited by anyone. This can be used for both personal and business uses, but it clearly is designed for those who want to manage a collaborative website. In a way this could be considered both a website and a blog, for it is continually evolving. Wetpaint is ad supported, extremely easy to use, and novices can get a feel for the service by adding to other people's sites before building their own. Wetpaint communities include fans of celebrities, TV shows, movies, bands, books, athletic groups, hobbies, chefs, animal lovers, technology lovers and more. One way to see what people gravitate to on Wetpaint is by checking out several of their top sites which are listed on the home page. There you'll get a sense of how it works, what others like, and maybe you'll find some great ideas to incorporate.

Some other fine choices:

Webnode – No ads, make as many sites as you want for free, very affordable upgrade to 3 GB bandwidth if wanted at just $3/month. http://www.webnode.com/

uCoz – 250 templates, custom domain name, 400MB storage, has ads but cheap upgrade to $3/month. http://www.ucoz.com/

Wix – 500 MB storage and 500 MB monthly bandwidth. Good for flash. Has Wix ads for free sites. http://www.wix.com/

Jimdo – 500 MB storage, ad supported. http://www.jimdo.com/

Remember, there are dozens of others I haven't listed and more are popping up all the time. Currently, I believe these are the best choices for the majority of people, although some may discover venues that work better for their needs. At the same time, the advice I give for one website will still work on another—you may just have to tweak the instructions a bit.

Plus there is another option. If you really want to build a free website entirely from scratch, as in without premade templates and site-building software, you can do that too. I only recommend this for people who are very computer savvy and like to challenge themselves and/or doing things their own way. For those interested, I'll explain this in more detail in the Other Things You Can Do chapter.

End of sample. The rest is available as ebook and paperback at major retailers.